Turnarounds:

Brains, Guts & Stamina

Peter McCann,

S. W. Dermer, Brian K. Hunter,

Ann MacDiarmid, Richard Morgan,

Mia Örndahl, Keith Robson & Fred Wagman

Illustrations by Alexandra Astafyeva & Crystal Dai

Order this book online at www.trafford.com/08-1470
or email orders@trafford.com

Most Trafford titles are also available at major online book retailers.

Note for Librarians: A cataloguing record for this book is available from Library and Archives Canada at www.collectionscanada.ca/amicus/index-e.html

Printed in Victoria, BC, Canada.

ISBN: 978-1-4251-9099-6

We at Trafford believe that it is the responsibility of us all, as both individuals and corporations, to make choices that are environmentally and socially sound. You, in turn, are supporting this responsible conduct each time you purchase a Trafford book, or make use of our publishing services. To find out how you are helping, please visit www.trafford.com/responsiblepublishing.html

Our mission is to efficiently provide the world's finest, most comprehensive book publishing service, enabling every author to experience success. To find out how to publish your book, your way, and have it available worldwide, visit us online at www.trafford.com/10510

www.trafford.com

North America & international
toll-free: 1 888 232 4444 (USA & Canada)
phone: 250 383 6864 • fax: 250 383 6804
email: info@trafford.com

The United Kingdom & Europe
phone: +44 (0)1865 487 395 • local rate: 0845 230 9601
facsimile: +44 (0)1865 481 507 • email: info.uk@trafford.com

10 9 8 7 6 5 4 3

TABLE OF CONTENTS

CHAPTER 1: CATCH A FALLING KNIFE

A Working Definition

A turnaround is a process to restore a failing company to sustainable competitive vitality. We will come back to this definition. For now, let's be clear: A turnaround must restore a failing company to competitive vitality. Stopping financial losses is good, but it's not enough. Paying down the bank is good, but it's not enough. Reducing costs is good, but it's not enough. A turnaround that does not restore a company to competitive vitality is a failed turnaround.

The reporter for the business section of an Ontario newspaper asked, "What is the difference between running a business well under normal conditions and doing a turnaround?" [1] The answer was: Turnarounds differ from managing a company well by the compression of time and the scarcity of resources. There's no time and scarce human and financial resources.

Far too often management and boards of directors cling to past impressions, false assumptions and vain hopes. As company performance slips, a company has fewer and fewer resources – less cash, less cash flow, less high caliber employees, maybe fewer customers. As a company has fewer and fewer resources, it has fewer and fewer strategic options. By the time that a Turnaround CEO or Consultant is hired, the company may be on a greased skateboard on the down ramp to the final exit.

Or, to use another metaphor, the Turnaround CEO is appointed to catch a falling knife. This book is about catching that falling knife. It is a complex, extremely stressful and often thankless and even reviled role. The authors have been Turnaround CEOs,

---

1 Meredith MacLeod of The Hamilton Spectator, interviewing Peter McCann. See Proactive Recession Planning, Page A16, The Hamilton Spectator, October 31, 2008.

executives, consultants and directors; we salute the Turnaround CEOs who show brains, guts and stamina.

Why Turnarounds Fail

Assuming that most failing companies attempt a turnaround, then successful turnarounds are unusual. "... the probability that a failing business will grow appreciably or become profitable within three years was less than 35 per cent." [2] In other words, it appears that 65% of turnarounds fail. It is self-evident that some of the failed turnarounds – some of the 65% of failing companies that did not turnaround – were not candidates for a turnaround. They had deteriorated beyond any reasonable prospect of recovery or there was a fundamental shift in the world: the classic buggy whip manufacturer facing a rapid mass adoption of the automobile, a disruptive technology. Perhaps in other cases timing was adverse – the turnaround started too late or the companies were caught in a severe recession or a major currency revaluation.

The balance of the failed turnarounds might have been successful turnarounds if managers trained in turnarounds had been given the authority by and support of their boards of directors or owners. How many could have been successful? As a wild guess, 50% of failing companies might have achieved a successful turnaround with better executive leadership and board support.

In the recession of the early 1990s the lead author did a series of consulting engagements for a major Canadian bank; the bank identified borrowers that it thought were failing and would likely go bankrupt. The bank demanded that the companies consent to a business review by a management consultant. The consultant presented management and turnaround consulting advice and written recommendations to the company and the bank. The consultant tracked the results: two years after the end of the business reviews, 72%

---

[2] Richard Foster and Sarah Kaplan, Creative Destruction: Why Companies That Are Built to Last Underperform the Market – and How to Successfully Transform them, New York: Currency, 2001; as quoted in The McKinsey Quarterly, 2006 Number 2, Page 66.

of those failing businesses were still in business and bank customers. Assuming that survival is a proxy for a successful turnaround, the successful turnaround rate of 72% can be fairly attributed to three parties: the bank was proactive, management was receptive, although not initially in most cases, and the consultant made a positive contribution. However, the companies that were subjected to the business review forced on them by the bank were not representative of all failing companies; the bank did not try to help those companies that it believed were either able to recover without professional assistance or beyond hope of recovery. Accordingly, the estimate that 50% of failing companies might achieve a successful turnaround may be reasonable.

Reasons for unsuccessful turnarounds

- Boards of directors, owners of privately held companies and senior managers ignore the death spiral of falling product competitiveness, falling profits and falling re-investment in products, processes, people and marketing until the companies become too enfeebled by losses and too entrenched in thinking and culture. They ignore the warning signs that are 'hiding in plain sight'. They react too late.

- Management when finally energized to take action are hobbled by past practices and past thinking, are reluctant to terminate commitments to unprofitable or declining products, processes, plants and divisions, cannot envisage new and innovative marketing and try to improve in small increments when large strides are required. Management trained to operate under normal conditions is not necessarily trained to do a turnaround – under conditions of compressed time and constrained resources. They react too timidly.

- Some companies must fail in order to make space in the competitive marketplace for new companies with new products and ideas. Each business failure is a loss for the owners and employees; but their loss is an opportunity for others. Each business failure liberates capital that is then redeployed by banks and suppliers to other, more efficient uses. A progressive capitalist society must have some business failures, as a forest must have old growth and new growth trees.

Organization of This Book

This book follows a simple plan. This chapter is an introduction to the book and the authors, guidance on reading and benefiting from the book, and some cautionary advice.

The second and third chapters provide an intellectual framework for looking at businesses, with an emphasis on distressed companies. We have all seen and heard both funny and serious stories of errors, accidents and disputes that only occurred because the individuals did not share common jargon. So, the chapters describe aspects of corporate performance and evaluation, and in later chapters these terms are used consistently. Material for these chapters and some material in later chapters were adapted from Strategy & Business Planning of Privately Held Companies, by Peter McCann [3].

The next several chapters take a sharper focus; they look at the generic characteristics of turnarounds and discuss some issues that must be addressed in virtually all turnarounds: people, marketing, operations, communications, strategy and financial restructurings. These chapters try to provide useful ideas and tools that have helped other Turnaround CEOs and Consultants.

Chapters 11 and 12 discuss the personal characteristics of brains, guts and stamina and provide advice on maintaining health during the siege. These two chapters are about the human being who faces and endures the challenges and stresses of a turnaround – the characteristics that contribute to success and approaches to maintaining personal health through the process of restoring corporate health.

The final chapter is a humanistic overview of turnarounds by someone who has studied the survivors.

---

[3] Available at www.trafford.com/00-0060.html

There is an overall consistency of message with variations in detail reflecting authors' experiences and professional perspectives. These variations in detail have not been edited out; the variations provide a spectrum of responses and views that will make the reader more informed and more nuanced in his or her choices and actions during a turnaround.

Case studies

The book has several case studies that describe real-world situations that the authors have been involved in. Some of the cases are heavily disguised but all are opportunities to consider how the advice in this book was applied successfully or unsuccessfully, and how matters might have been managed differently. If you want a faster read with mostly theory and mostly detailed guidance, read the chapters and skip the cases. If you prefer a more leisurely read with pauses to think and reflect on other people's experiences, read the chapters and case studies in the order they appear.

Authorship

There are several authors who have contributed to this book. Extracts from their profiles and resumes are at the back of this book. Peter McCann, the lead author, is a management consultant and Turnaround Consultant. He is the author of Strategy & Business Planning of Privately Held Companies.

Dr. S. W. Dermer, MD, FRCP(C), Occupational Psychiatric Consultant, is a widely respected psychiatrist with an interest in managerial and workplace mental health and a concern for justice in the workplace. Stan was persuaded to offer some brief words of guidance and advice.

Brian K. Hunter has over 30 years of commercial lending and venture capital investing experience, spanning many industries and a couple of recessions. Brian has seen and participated in numerous financial restructurings of troubled companies.

Ann MacDiarmid is a seasoned communications and crisis management professional who has contributed a chapter on communications as well as provided valuable and insightful comments that have made this book better.

Rick Morgan has about forty years in advertising and marketing with successive iterations of a large Canadian advertising agency. He has worked with a wide spectrum of large and small companies across the industrial and commercial landscape.

Mia Örndahl is a Finnish academic and consultant who brings a humanistic view to this discussion of turnarounds based on her research with the survivors of turnarounds. The hard-driving, numerate approach to turnarounds must be tempered by a humanistic view. Accordingly, it's appropriate that Mia Örndahl's comments conclude this book.

Keith Robson, Fred Wagman and Peter McCann have contributed case studies from their turnaround experiences – a small sample of their extensive experience. Fred, Keith and Peter are battle-tested in turnarounds and have over one hundred years of combined business experience (and if one wrote how many years over one hundred it would be embarrassing).

History of this book

Books are rivers formed by streams merging and swelling the flow. This book is the result of several streams. Obviously, 'Strategy & Business Planning of Privately Held Companies' by Peter McCann, published in 2000, dealt with turnarounds as well as other corporate positions; it is perhaps the source stream. In July 2008 Mia Örndahl in Finland and Peter McCann in Canada started discussions by email on collaboration and continued those discussions in late August in Helsinki. In August Keith Robson and Peter McCann started talking about doing a seminar on turnarounds, and continued those discussions with Fred Wagman to the point that a seminar was prepared and presented by Fred and Peter in early November 2008. Meanwhile, Mia and Peter had discussed several ideas involving collaboration and by September 2008 Peter had raised the idea of a book with Keith. Keith's ideas, encouragement and comments were helpful as this book was written. More streams of insight flowed into the river when Stan Dermer, Rick Morgan, Ann MacDiarmid and Brian Hunter joined the discussions with Peter and agreed to contribute their expertise. The final stream that contributed to the book was the heavy rain of bad economic news that flooded the United States in mid-2008 and the world by late 2008.

Get Legal Advice

Rather than repeat warnings in chapter after chapter, let's cover an essential caution. This book is not a substitute for legal advice; spend the money early to save a ton of money and grief later. Numerous topics have legal aspects, and the best legal advice (and you should only want the best legal advice) will be based on the facts of the particular situation and on the laws and jurisprudence of the jurisdiction. So, hire the best available lawyer. Hire a good corporate lawyer who will be helpful and even invaluable in certain creditor negotiations. Hire a good labor lawyer who will become your trusted confidante. If a proposal under your country's bankruptcy laws is a possibility, meet with a bankruptcy lawyer – knowing the options is part of choosing the right option. If environmental issues are a potential issue, hire an environmental lawyer.

Now, a caution about lawyers: lawyers give legal, negotiating and business advice, and they may not explicitly state the nature of the advice that they are giving. So, when your lawyer says 'you should do this', ask if that is legal, negotiating or business advice. If your trusted lawyer has given you legal advice, follow it. If the advice is negotiating advice, listen and discuss but remember that you probably know far more about the psychology and finances of a particular negotiation. If the advice is business advice, listen attentively but remember that you are the business executive. Your reputation and employment is on the line.

Professional Assistance

This book can be used as a guide to the turnaround of mildly troubled companies; however, even mildly troubled companies have unique problems. Each author has provided generalized advice based on years of experience and appropriate for many turnarounds; however, specific turnarounds have specific characteristics that require specific responses. If even seasoned turnaround professionals consult with legal, accounting, banking, human resource, marketing, engineering and other professionals, then you should, too. The professional advisers during a turnaround should not – in most cases – be the current advisers. Current advisers have views shaped by their historical knowledge of a company and its environment, and that knowledge may be stale and inaccurate. Their views may be too respectful of the status quo or entrenched management. Current auditors and legal firms may be retained, if the Turnaround CEO has confidence in them; but there is merit in at least actively considering alternatives or at least limiting the incumbent advisers' involvement in the turnaround. Hiring a Turnaround CEO or a Turnaround Consultant should be at least considered.

Final Advice

A turnaround is a process to restore a failing company to sustainable competitive vitality. As Mia Örndahl points out later in this book, the Finnish recession in the early 1990s was brutally severe; companies did fail but other companies survived and in time prospered. Turnarounds can be achieved even in very hostile environments. As a Turnaround CEO or Turnaround Consultant you will have hours and days of bad news, seemingly malevolent opposition and bone-weary fatigue. Your brains, guts and stamina will be tested beyond any reasonable limits; but you will be sustained by a deep conviction that a turnaround can be achieved and that you can make it happen.

Beware of the crush of unrealistic expectations of immediate, dramatic results. Don't let a panicked board of directors or lenders spread their panic to you; urgency is important; panic is awful. Through the grinding stress and the iron determination, remember that the company and its employees and shareholders will never love you. The turnaround is a vital job, but it is only a job. Your health and your spouse and children are far more important. Never sacrifice your health, spouse and children. Remember that, and you will survive as a human being no matter what occurs during a turnaround.

CASE STUDY: THE SMALL CITY ART GALLERY[4]

The City

The Small City Art Gallery (SCAG) was located in a city with a population of approximately 350,000.

Illustration: Crystal Dai

The city was considered "blue collar" because of its large historical dependence on the industrial sector; however, by 2008, employment in the city's universities, colleges and schools was larger than industrial employment and the city was noticeably more gentrified.

Governance

SCAG was governed by a twenty-six member board of directors. Sixteen of the board members were dilettantes who loved appearing in the society pages; they had little governance or business experience. Three board members were art historians. Six were people who felt they needed to add culture to their resumes. In 2006 SCAG's Executive Director was the remaining board member. He had been the SCAG administrator for twenty years.

---

[4] © Peter McCann, 2008; adapted from a case he prepared in 2000 for use at Khazar University, School of Economics and Management, Baku, Azerbaijan.

Financial Performance

In 2006, SCAG had three revenue sources, totaling about $2,000,000: interest from its endowment fund (12%), proceeds from its annual fund raising drive (38%) and government grants (50%). Revenues on an inflation-adjusted basis were constant from 1980 to 2005; however, the donor base had changed. The number of individual donors had decreased 15% and the average individual donation had decreased 5%. Corporate donations had increased by 35%, absorbing both the decline in individual donations and inflation. SCAG had three major expense categories: fund raising and administration (37%), art education (7%), and art exhibitions (56%). Buying art was off budget, as acquisitions of art were usually due to donations from individual collectors. Labor expenses, being the largest component of each expense category, had risen faster than revenues. Influential board members insisted on maintaining the frequency and scope of SCAG's exhibitions and insisted on balanced budgets. Therefore, the non-labor components of fund raising, administration and art education had shrunk during the previous twenty years.

Executive Directors

In early 2006, the board of directors decided that it needed a strategic plan. The Executive Director was instructed to prepare a strategic plan. He consulted with every member of the board, set up a board sub-committee and a SCAG staff committee and studied several books on strategic planning. By late 2006, there was no strategic plan and the board fired the Director. A new Executive Director was quickly hired in early 2007. This Executive Director agreed with the prevailing board opinion that the primary business for SCAG was art exhibitions. The new Executive Director went through a quick consultative process, and submitted a mission statement for board approval. It was approved in April 2007. In summary the new mission statement said: “We exhibit great art for the masses.” Still no strategic plan had been created or taken to the board.

On the basis of the newly approved mission statement, SCAG de-emphasized art education and emphasized great art exhibited in an elitist environment. Corporate sponsors reduced or eliminated their support. Popular support had slipped and further dropped after the implementation of the mission statement. Individual donations of small amounts decreased. Therefore, SCAG faced a significant revenue shortfall, and since popular support had eroded, the local government was reluctant to increase support for SCAG. By mid 2008, SCAG's expenses exceeded the total of revenues from all sources. The capital in the endowment fund was being used to pay operating expenses. For the second time in two years, the Executive Director was fired and the board advertised in Canadian newspapers for a new Executive Director.

Michele Prentice was hired in November 2008 to turnaround SCAG. Prentice had grown up in Toronto and had been educated in art history in Montreal and Frankfurt, Germany. After six years as Executive Director of an innovative artists' co-operative in Vancouver, she had accepted the position as Executive Director of SCAG knowing that she had her work cut out for her. The board believed that Prentice had the skills and determination to achieve a turnaround.

Commentary on the case study

This brief case study gives a simple example of what a turnaround CEO may be thrust into and it shows some of the common elements that contribute to a turnaround. The board was too large and too unskilled. There was an inherent conflict in the strategic goals of 'art for the masses' and 'great art exhibited in an elitist environment.' Financial performance had deteriorated. SCAG was consuming its endowment fund (roughly equivalent in some ways to a company's equity) to fund operating losses. Popular support (equivalent to a company's customer base) was down. Michele Prentice faced many of the same urgent questions that bedevil Turnaround CEOs. What are the key problems? What are the key opportunities? What resources does she have or might reasonably expect to acquire? Who are most likely to be helpful? Who are likely to be impediments to progress? What should she do immediately and over the first six months? Later chapters and case studies will show what strategies and tactics can be used.

CHAPTER 2: POSITIONS, PRINCIPLES & PARADIGMS

Not Every Flu Is Pneumonia

There are lots of big and small problems in life – and very few real disasters. And, sometimes, it's hard to know how significant a problem really is. So, it's prudent to invest time and effort to determine whether or not a company is in a turnaround position.

Positions

This chapter starts with the five basic company positions. The descriptions will suffice to identify the position of most companies. People are not unequivocally extroverted or introverted, cerebral or emotional; nonetheless, a person may be fairly labeled by various characteristics if those characteristics are dominant. Companies are the same. Companies may be fairly characterized as being in one of the five positions if the characteristics of a position are dominant. Knowing a company's position helps to narrow the range of issues to be researched and analyzed. This will help the Turnaround CEO confirm whether or not his or her specific company is, in fact, in a turnaround situation, or is in better or worse condition. Each of the five basic positions of corporate vitality describes a cluster of interrelated characteristics. Characteristics include a company's financial and non-financial resources and capacity to grow, adapt and compete. Obviously, a company with positive characteristics has more attractive choices than a company with negative characteristics. To provide further help to define a company's position, there is a questionnaire included in the Appendices.

<u>Go For Gold</u>

Go For Gold companies are not perfect companies; but, they know what's important and they do all the important things well and some important things superbly. They excel at either marketing or operations, and are good at the other. They know what they do well and they focus on doing it better. They focus on their strengths. Their industries may be embryonic, growing or mature; but their industries are not dying. Financial results are strong. Earnings are re-invested in planned growth. Cost control systems are up-to-date and are used by management. Productivity and performance measurements are tracked and monitored. Overheads are appropriate to company needs. Strategic goals determine capital expenditures. Shareholders demand performance appropriate to the maturity of the company and industry. Management has a vision of excellence and market domination. Management accepts risk as being inherent in progress and growth but has a clear sense of the acceptable level of risk. Staff who share the vision and contribute to their companies' success are appreciated and rewarded with money, challenges and security.

Status Quo

Status Quo companies are living on the benefits of past achievements, harvesting yesterday's efforts and investments. They may be in mature industries that have not yet been ravaged by an innovative player. They may not have kept pace with industry gains in quality and productivity, but the lag may be moderate and thus not a major disadvantage at the moment. Status Quo companies may be owned and managed by a president who worked many years to build the company and is now worn-out, risk adverse and out-of-touch with current competitive conditions. Or, they may be owned by a family with management vested in the second or third generation, which may attempt to perpetuate antiquated business practices, or a hired administrator who may seek the illusion of stability by risk avoidance (instead of risk management). The board of directors may be old family friends or family members, and everyone has grown old and tired together. Good performance is considered to be the avoidance of losses and, perhaps, the payment of token dividends. Financial results are mediocre. Revenues and earnings may have been stable or slightly declining (especially on an inflation-adjusted basis) for several years. However, working capital and debt / equity ratios may be strong as earnings are accumulated as cash or applied as reductions of debt rather than used for expansion or dividends. Capital expenditures may be for replacement of assets rather than improvement of the company's products or cost structure. Overheads may be excessive due to reluctance to deal with under-performing products, divisions and individuals. Status Quo companies appreciate established practices and relationships.

Frugality may dominate because it is a safe principle: there is little risk in saving money. Overall, Status Quo companies are not in bad shape; there is time to make the right changes the right way.

Tune Up

Tune Up companies are too healthy to die, too sick to prosper. Cash flow may be insufficient for investment in new technology. Overheads are probably high. Management may not have kept pace with accelerating requirements for sophisticated business acumen, product quality and productivity. Tune Up companies may be in industries that are growing or stable; however, they may rapidly reach a crisis if a new industry player or technology intensifies competition. They may not know their customers and likely use a stale marketing strategy; but they may still have some customer loyalty or brand awareness. Products may have been surpassed by the products of several competitors. Research & development and marketing may be spread over too many products, with the result that no product has been adequately rejuvenated. The shareholders, boards of directors, management and staff may have an undefined sense that some change is required. Accordingly, a meaningful, permanent attitude shift may be easier to achieve in Tune Up companies than in Status Quo companies. Overall, Tune Up companies may have some building blocks of success, such as an established customer base, adequate products and management and staff with the potential to be re-energized and re-focused.

Turnaround

Turnaround companies are on a collision course with bankruptcy. Turnaround companies may have operating losses, decreasing equity and weak working capital. Suppliers and especially the bank may be nervous and may try to reduce their exposure. In severe cases, paying the payroll may be a problem. Turnaround companies in healthy, growing industries can often be saved. Companies in declining industries may face the double obstacles of internal problems and intensifying competitive pressures on pricing and margins. Companies in rapidly growing industries may face the double obstacles of internal problems and intensifying competitive pressures to achieve technological and quality leadership. Conversely, turnaround companies which are fundamentally sound but which have incurred substantial loses due to an unsuccessful technological leap, an acquisition or a major expansion ('bet the company and lost') may be saved by the simple expedients of ending the mistake ('cutting the losses') and, perhaps, attracting additional equity investment. Shareholders and management may be overwhelmed by the problems, dispirited by past errors and failures and paralyzed by fear that further mistakes might cause irreparable damage. Accordingly, some Turnaround companies sink into the Exit position and drift into oblivion. In other cases, management may panic and make radical changes in products or customer and supplier relationships in order to gain temporary cash flow improvements at the sacrifice of medium and longer-term viability.

Exit

The obvious Exit companies have large operating losses, negative working capital and equity, obsolete products, weak staff and inadequate management. In short, these companies are a waste of scarce economic resources and speedy closure will minimize losses to suppliers, lenders and owners. Closure may be by voluntary liquidation or by bankruptcy. There is another category of Exit companies: profitable companies in a declining industry or companies without the financial or managerial resources to compete in a rapidly changing industry. These Exit companies may be sold to stronger competitors, suppliers or customers or they may be phased out over many months. Of the five positions, the Exit position is the hardest for shareholders and executives to accept intellectually and emotionally. Procrastination concerning an exit decision when a company is, truly, in the Exit position may result in large operating losses and less recovery of equity when the exit decision is finally made and implemented. Shareholders of Exit companies should be cautious of advice from staff that 'the business will improve' and cautious about family considerations such as providing on-going employment for family members. Diagnosing Exit companies requires professional insight and objectivity. Call an independent professional (not the company's current accountancy or legal firm) to discuss and review the diagnosis. Do not implement an exit strategy without professional assistance (which may be from the company's current accountancy or legal firm).

A checklist to double check

A few years ago the lead author was on a plane from Toronto to London on route to Kazakhstan, and a businessman from Ontario, Canada told him that on one of his overseas trips he called home and his teenage son answered and was especially warm and friendly, and then abruptly said 'Dad, remember the Toyota?' Think about that – five thousand kilometers away – too far to know the facts, but certain that bad news was coming! Of course, the businessman was able to ask questions and establish that the car was a wreck but no one was hurt. So, when confronted with bad news, ask questions. The Appendices have a handy questionnaire with 145 questions as an additional tool to estimate the company's position. Completing the questionnaire is a good idea for two reasons. First, the questionnaire will help distinguish between a Turnaround and a non-Turnaround situation, and thus will help guide thinking to appropriate responses and help avoid inappropriate responses. Second, the questionnaire will categorize issues so that the Turnaround CEO or Consultant can see the magnitude and clustering of issues. So, complete the questionnaire, either at this point in reading the book, or after finishing the book but before launching a concerted turnaround effort.

The banker's test

By this point you have looked at your actual or hypothetical situation with the tools of your insights and experience, the categorization indicated by the descriptions of the positions and the questionnaire. There is another strong indicator: your commercial bankers and lenders. If your bankers are nervous or less supportive, you have a problem. The obvious problem is that your bankers may restrict credit. The underlying problem is corporate performance. Almost every businessperson bashes and criticizes banks and bankers; but, bankers have a good track record about objectively assessing commercial borrowers – they certainly are not always right, but they are right often enough that shareholders and executives should listen very attentively when bankers start asking probing, uncomfortable questions. Those questions are a strong sign that the company is entering Turnaround territory. If the company's banker thinks that it is in a Turnaround position, it likely is. Companies that do not listen and react effectively move downscale towards the Exit position.

Principles

Turnarounds are guided or shaped by fear, greed or principles. Turnarounds are chaotic, and fear and greed are rampant; inevitably, bad decisions result if the Turnaround CEO and the entire company are not deeply anchored by fundamental principles. The fundamental principles are Ethics, Focus, Excellence, Frugality and Urgency. The principles should be part of a total business perspective and be influential in every decision. No principle, except Ethics, should so dominate decision-making as to suppress the other principles.

Ethics

Ethics are not in short supply. Many ethical errors are not due to malice or greed; the errors are due to executives swamped by activities and demands on their time and so rushed that they do not take the time to think through issues and implications. Some supposed ethical errors are, on closer examination, not ethical failures but rather honestly held differences in opinion concerning, for example, environmental issues and investments in countries governed by repressive regimes. Of course, ethical lapses and violations do occur, but the fact that violations of ethics are disturbing indicates that the business community does have a deep sense of ethics. Occasionally, executives wrap themselves in the cloak of self-righteousness, masking procrastination and befuddlement. Do not confuse ethics with mushiness. Executives must have the guts to make difficult and even unpopular decisions.

Focus

Focus recognizes that we cannot satisfy all the world's customers, we cannot make all the world's products and we cannot seize all the world's opportunities. In a highly competitive world, a company must focus on its core customers and core products, or its customers will be lured away by aggressive competitors with newer products and superior marketing. It takes managerial talent and money to compete, and diversification dilutes both.

Excellence

Excellence is exceeding customers' expectations. Excellence is an attitude and a personal value system. Companies expect excellence from their suppliers, although they themselves may not especially strive to give excellence. Excellence and quality are, in many instances, used interchangeably but they are subtly different. Excellence looks outward to customers' expectations (although the 'customer' may be another department or assembly plant of the same company). Quality looks inward to the company's products and processes. Quality initiatives should be used to serve excellence; quality is not a substitute for excellence. Quality can be measured, precisely and reliably. Savings of 5% to 12% are often attributed to intelligent efforts to improve quality. Excellence, on the other hand, is less easily measured; but measurement of excellence may be approximated on the basis of comparative price, quality and customer satisfaction.

Frugality

To be frugal, a company must know its costs, and most executives do not really know their costs. Business people rely on their financial statements; however, financial statements remain largely a report to legitimately interested parties, such as shareholders, lenders and governments. Management, on the other hand, needs information to make rational operational decisions. Getting operationally useful information is management's responsibility, not the auditors. The frugal company will always ask if there is a different total expenditure that will produce both excellence and greater financial returns.

Urgency

Businesses with a sense of urgency almost always are more successful. They identify and seize opportunities. When they make mistakes, they act quickly and decisively to correct their mistakes. Urgency is being aware that the hostile environment will probably worsen. Executives must manage within a hostile, intensely competitive environment; Turnaround CEOs function in a heightened state of tension beyond the norm. Leaders do not freeze in the face of challenge. Urgency is not an excuse for reliance on intuition at the expense of sound research and analysis or shoddy preparation leading to flawed implementation. Urgency should not be confused with vigorous pursuit of a wrong, hastily identified objective. Urgency is acting decisively on the best available information.

Non-exclusive list of principles

The preceding list of principles is non-exclusive. There are other principles that other people would advocate with considerable justification. A strong argument has been made that Transparency should be included. As Ann MacDiarmid has written: "Turnarounds with secrets just don't work." Elsewhere she has emphasized the importance of transparency of facts. Transparency is prominent both in Ann MacDiarrmid's chapter on communications and in Mia Örndahl's chapter summing up a humanistic view of turnarounds. The counter-arguments of CEOs and litigation lawyers would be that certain facts such as threats of forced liquidation by lenders or regulatory violations would be de-stabilizing and potentially ruinous in the event of litigation. The debate on the inclusion of Transparency could be protracted; however, it is certain that Transparency is highly desirable.

Paradigms

Turnaround CEOs cannot work in an intellectual vacuum; they must be able to organize their own thoughts and must impose a disciplined structure on the torrent of bad news, conflicting data and unreasonable demands. A paradigm is a pattern or intellectual framework that shapes perceptions and actions. Reliance on a single paradigm may be simplistic but the seven paradigms together provide a holistic approach to management.

Microeconomic paradigm

This paradigm states that industry structure, technology and company specific knowledge drive conduct which drives performance. It is a powerful tool for examining performance and strategic options.

Accountants' paradigm

The accountants' paradigm states that understanding revenues and expenses is mandatory to understanding business. Common techniques to identify many symptoms and some causes of corporate performance include analysis of revenues, expenses, profits, assets, liabilities and asset and expense ratios. Over-reliance on the accountants' paradigm can lead to treating the symptoms and not the causes of performance. Nonetheless, neglect of the accountants' paradigm is a more common problem than over reliance on it. In fact, failure to understand the numbers is an early warning sign of a possible business failure. For many privately held companies, sophisticated financial techniques are rarely required or available; but understanding the basic numbers is always essential.

Marketing paradigm

The marketing paradigm is about satisfying customers profitably. It is about the basics: product, price, promotion, place, customer, channel of distribution, contribution margin and, definitely, profit. It is a useful tool to identify some of the causes of under-performance and to indicate possible remedial actions. Some companies have suffered due to marketing thinking and methods that may have been productive at one time but that became stale and unproductive over the years.

Operations paradigm

The operations paradigm creates value. It is about making and delivering customer satisfaction - through purchasing, manufacturing, logistics, research and development, products, processes, quality and cost effectiveness. The study of operations as a distinct discipline started with manufacturing. The tools of modern operations management are now applied to distributors (vehicle utilization planning), banks (efficient credit card processing), restaurants (food flow in kitchens), hospitals (purchasing and inventory management) and accounting firms (audit scheduling). Generally, companies in mature industries should progress by making a steady stream of small, inexpensive process improvements that are consistent with corporate resources and supportive of corporate strategy. Incrementalism will not overwhelm managerial or financial resources and may yield better returns on investment than expensive and complex solutions.

Technology paradigm

The technology paradigm creates progress. It is the search for the application of science and engineering to solve mundane and complex issues. It is new equipment to do things faster, better and cheaper. It is applied to operations, marketing and administration. It has been said that when technologically primitive people first saw airplanes they thought the planes were gods; some companies seem to think that new technologies are gods capable of solving their problems without managerial intervention. Wiser companies view technology as enhancers of human capabilities. Few privately held companies can aspire to technology innovation; but they can strive for competency.

Organization behavior paradigm

The organizational behavior paradigm states that the right organizational structure with the right people and congruence between reward systems, employee behavior and corporate goals will produce the right results. This is the most theoretical paradigm. It is difficult to apply successfully because corporate goals and needs, people and the effectiveness of reward systems change through time. Over-reliance on the organizational behavior paradigm may lead to corporate self-absorption and self-indulgent introspection - too many career planning seminars, morale and team building dynamics workshops and diversity and sensitivity training and too few customer service evaluations, warranty claims analysis and product defect reduction programs. However, neglect of the organizational behavior paradigm is a more common problem. Senior executives may prefer a tax audit or a dental appointment to an afternoon assessing corporate training needs or an employee performance appraisal. Even obviously simple issues may have an underlying organizational behavior dimension that may furnish the solution or part of the solution.

Managerial preferences paradigm

The managerial preferences paradigm states that business decisions are made on the basis of facts and financial, marketing and technology projections as evaluated and interpreted by managers within the context of their desires and visions. Decisions that may not appear rational to objective observers may be understandable in the context of a manager's vision. Managerial preferences drive the choice of objectives and the pace and nature of efforts to achieve the objectives. Preferences can be very basic: we are in the car rental business, gladiola farming or astrophysics book publishing. Managerial preferences unchecked by reality and ethics can lead to disaster; preferences must be consistent with the external environment and with corporate capabilities. The external environment includes market demand, available technology, competition and regulation. Corporate capabilities include financial resources, staff skills and managerial talent.

Balance among the paradigms

Successful firms achieve consistency amongst the paradigms and congruence with the external environment. In athletics, we know that a muscle imbalance can lead to injury: overdeveloped quadriceps may strain underdeveloped hamstrings. In business, a paradigm imbalance can lead to injury: a dominance of marketing over operations can lead to overspending on marketing and a neglect of product and process improvements. The most striking imbalance is seen in cases of the managerial preferences paradigm dominating all other considerations. The Turnaround CEO must quickly identify and start to correct imbalances amongst the paradigms and incongruities with the external environment.

I MARINE SUPPLIES [5]

Illustration: Crystal Dai

business. Leo and Jasmine had married when they were 22 years old. Their five sons had all served customers and when they were old enough to get a driver's license, they drove trucks to suppliers and delivered boats, motors and fuel to customers.

The children were adults now. The eldest was a teacher in the nearby city. Pascal was an MBA graduate and a commercial loan manager with a major bank in another Canadian province. Milos, the next eldest, had worked in the family business for 18 years since he had finished high school. He was very active in many community and regional projects. Charles was also a teacher. Tim, the youngest, had worked in the family business for 8 years since he had finished high school.

The Tegovski Business

Tegovski Marine Supplies Ltd. sold small sailboats and motorboats for fishing, water-skiing and cruising. The area was thinly populated and was bordered by a river on the

---

[5] © by Peter McCann; adapted from a case that he prepared in 2000 for use at Khazar University, School of Economics and Management, Baku, Azerbaijan.

west and low mountains on the east. Per capita income in the area was about 78% of the Canadian average. Downriver was a large Canadian city.

Tegovski bought almost 100% of its inventory and supplies from Downrigger Boating Organization ('DBO'). DBO was owned by about 190 independent marine supplies retailers, including Tegovski, from across Canada. DBO was professionally managed. It acted as a purchasing agent, buying from boat and engine manufacturers at large discounts. DBO charged a purchasing fee, plus an advertising fee (to pay for DBO's national advertising) and a mandatory surcharge that was used to buy shares in DBO. The shares could not be redeemed, except when an owner of a business sold the business. If a business went bankrupt, the shares were cancelled and the investment was deducted from the account payable to DBO.

1983 – 1999: The Business Grows

In 1983 Leo borrowed $15,000 (in inflation-adjusted 2004 dollars) from a bank and established a tiny marine supply business in Carterville. Leo had nominal equity in the beginning and money was always a problem. He worked selling in the store and delivering to customers. Jasmine worked in the store and did the bookkeeping on the kitchen table at night. The store was a wood-frame building about 20 square meters (about 200 square feet). The store and the land were rented. Gradually, business improved. In 1991 Tegovski Building Supplies bought the land that it had rented and built a large cement block store.

1996 – Buy A Competitor

The closest competitors were two marine supply businesses in Simpsonville. One of the two businesses was a long established, well-run family business. The second Simpsonville business went into bankruptcy in 1996 due to its heavy debt load. The bank that had financed the bankrupt Simpsonville business offered to sell the assets to Tegovski. After lengthy negotiations, Tegovski bought the land, building, inventory and equipment of the bankrupt Simpsonville business and modernized the store. The expansion was financed by short-term debt from Tegovski's bank and a 15-year mortgage from another bank. Tegovski Marine Supplies continued to be marginally profitable, despite the much heavier debt load.

1997 – 2001 – More Expansion & Change in Shareholdings

In 1997 Tegovski borrowed more money from the bank and tripled the size of the store. In 1999 the company bought an old building in Carterville, renovated it and leased it to a group of physicians who used it as a clinic. The 'doctors' building', as Leo called it, cost $150,000 and was financed by a mortgage of $115,000 and working capital. Tegovski Marine Supplies lost money in 2000, and recovered to profitability in 2001. Cash continued to be a problem. In 2001 ownership was restructured so that Leo owned 25%, Milos owned 50% and Tim owned 25%. Milos and Tim did not pay for their shares but they agreed that the business would pay Leo and Jasmine a salary for life. There was a Shareholders' Agreement that obligated Milos and Tim to vote their shares in agreement with Leo's vote.

2002 – Buy Another Competitor

In late 2001 a competitor in Castleford, a small town north of Simpsonville, went bankrupt after several years of declining sales. Tegovski decided to buy the assets.

May 20, 2002 request for financing

> The transaction involves the purchase of real estate, fixtures and equipment, and vehicles at a total cost, subject to inventory counts, of $260,000. After the transaction Tegovski Marine Supplies will build a modern storage shed, buy another truck for $18,000, increase inventory by an additional $100,000 to a level comparable to the company's other stores, and gradually increase receivables to $70,000. The forecast increase in inventory and receivables reflects the company's fiscal 2002 ratios and a projected increase in sales of $600,000.

The commercial bank and the federal bank approved financing, and Tegovski bought the assets of the Castleford company, excluding accounts receivable, in August 2002, and completed the expansion in Castleford in April 2003.

During 2002 and 2003 Tegovski was the main supplier of marine supplies for the expansion of a government fresh water research institute in Simpsonville. Sales for the expansion of the institute were $250,000 in 2003 and $600,000 in 2004.

Management Issues

Leo continued to be President but he took less and less day-to-day interest in operations. He drove trucks on deliveries and served customers in the store. Jasmine continued to work in sales. Milos was the effective General Manager, although he was busy with his many community activities. Tim was named Store Manager in Castleford in the hope that increased responsibility would motivate him to work harder. Relations between Leo, Milos and Tim were strained. In February 2004 Leo wrote a 12-page memo to Milos. The memo criticized Milos's ideas to improve profitability and his level of community activism. Leo's memo suggested that the business be divided: Leo would take one store, Milos would take the second store, and Tim would take the third and smallest store. Leo and Milos alternated between arguing for hours and not talking for days.

Spring, 2004

By 2004 the competitive environment was changing as an American company built large marine supply stores in major cities across Canada, including the city nearest Tegovski's three stores, and advertised extensively in newspapers, radio and television.

In early May 2004 DBO's regional manager met with Leo and Milos and stressed that DBO was unhappy with Tegovski's slow payment of its account payable. In late May 2004 Leo was asked to meet with the commercial bank. The bank's commercial loans manager and his regional vice-president explained that the bank was concerned about the financial performance of Tegovski Marine Supplies Ltd.. The bank reluctantly agreed to lend up to $550,000 during fiscal 2005. The bank required that Leo, Milos and Tim sign full personal guarantees of all current and future bank loans. By June 2004, Leo Tegovski was feeling old, tired, discouraged and depressed. He did not know what he could do, should do or wanted to do.

Balance Sheet & Cash Flow Data

		2001	2002	2003	2004
Sales	$	2,034,982	1,945,587	2,464,007	2,815,527
Sales / total assets		137.7%	115.6%	106.5%	129.8%
Working capital		$453,857	$443,133	$564,396	$469,514
Working capital ratio		1.88	1.80	1.69	1.68
Total debts		1,038,210	1,157,113	1,770,011	1,637,796
Equity & shareholder loans		440,128	525,521	544,033	530,518
Debts / equity		2.36	2.20	3.25	3.09
Bank line as % of Rec. + Inv.		32.4%	31.0%	31.0%	39.5%
Net cash from operations	$	26,064	97,035	57,701	66,013
- as % of retail sales		1.3%	5.0%	2.3%	2.3%
- as % of equity		5.9%	18.5%	10.6%	12.4%
Net income	$	18,618	86,193	2,418	28,126
Amortization		38,345	42,430	62,350	79,381
Gain on disposal of capital assets			-32,388	-23,161	-10,617
Dividends in the year					-10,764
Shareholders loans - increase		-30,899	800	16,094	-20,113
Net cash from operations		26,064	97,035	57,701	66,013
Increase in term debt		-89,943	-34,913	341,831	15,841
Increase in DBO Shares		15,793	22,591	20,131	21,700
Net capital expenditures		15,517	164,492	266,584	125,256
Net cash from operations		26,064	97,035	57,701	66,013
Pay principal on term debt		-89,943	-34,913	341,831	15,841
Pay for capital expenditures		-15,517	-164,492	-266,584	-125,256
Pay for DBO shares		-15,793	-22,591	-20,131	-21,700
Cash available for working capital		-95,189	-124,961	112,817	-65,102

Commentary on the case

A useful approach when starting a turnaround is to apply the preceding discussion of paradigms, principles and positions to develop at least a preliminary analysis of the situation and, thus, form ideas on what actions are required. A consultant engaged by Tegovski Marine Supplies Ltd. might start with an analysis that would include each paradigm and principle and all the information available. Under the heading of Accountants' Paradigm there should be an analysis of historical revenue and expense patterns. The revenues, expenses, assets and liabilities of the 'doctors building' should be listed separately so that the profitability and return on equity of marine supplies and the real estate investment over the preceding years can be seen. The sales to the fresh water institute should be separated, so that a normalized income statement is calculated to show the sustainable level of earnings. The normalized income statement should then be the basis of a three year forecast if Tegovski makes no structural changes; there should be three versions of the 'no change' forecast: no impact from new competition, a low impact from new competition, and medium-high impact from new competition. There should also be a series of forecasts or scenarios to test or model various options such as consolidating three stores into one store.

In this instance, the managerial preferences paradigm obviously deserves extra attention: the work commitment and the motivations of Leo, Milos, Tim and Jasmine are different, and different behaviors are exhibited. It would appear that there is a stalemate in decision-making and an absence of both leadership and followership. Resolution of the business situation may depend on prior resolution of the interpersonal dynamics.

There should be the same thoroughness in the analysis under the headings of each of the other paradigms. While there is too little information in the case to enable definitive comments, the closure of a series of competitors indicates that attention should be devoted to the evolving structure of the industry. It may be that the industry is undergoing consolidation and rationalization that will lead to economies of scale in operations and purchasing for the larger survivors. If so, it would be reasonable to question if the Tegovski business can survive unless it expands by acquiring additional locations or consolidates its existing locations into a single, larger and more efficient location.

The same methodology and thoroughness can be applied with the principles. The case does not give enough information to justify definitive comments on, for example, Frugality; however, a Turnaround CEO will be able to accumulate enough information over the first few weeks to make a fairly complete survey of the issues and to complete a preliminary assessment. That assessment will guide the Turnaround CEO in the selection of the most promising alternatives.

Experienced Turnaround CEOs may do their analysis in a less formal, structured manner. Less experienced Turnaround CEOs should make time to record and summarize their observations and analysis. An actual or hypothetical report to the board of directors is highly useful in developing and articulating a coherent vision for the turnaround.

CHAPTER 3: ALTERNATIVES, ESSENTIALS & PHASES

Every morning when the Turnaround CEO wakes, he or she will make an explicit or implicit decision to continue the turnaround or not. On a risk adjusted basis, is it prudent to continue to operate the company? Are the probable shareholder returns sufficient to compensate for the possible losses? Every astute Turnaround CEO and Consultant is aware of the choice; it is lurking in the shadows of every early morning.

The commitment to turnaround a company is not irreversible; in fact, that implicit or explicit commitment to a turnaround was made based on numerous assumptions. New information will inevitably emerge: competitors may launch superior products, aggressive marketing or price wars; violations of environmental or health & safety regulations may be identified such that the risk of continuance to the officers and directors would be prohibitive; or, a recession may start before the benefits of a turnaround can be realized. Therefore, it is vital to be open to new information and to have a contingency plan.

Once the company is stabilized at or above breakeven, a decision should be made either to move into a recovery and growth mode of a complete turnaround, or to sell the business. The recovery and growth phase will include repairing morale, expanding profitable product lines, possibly some market re-positioning or product re-engineering, and probably some financial re-engineering involving term financing, equity injections or debt to equity swaps by suppliers. The recovery and growth phase may last two or more years, and will not be completed until the business achieves sustainable competitive vitality. Because the recovery and growth phase is so arduous and lengthy, shareholders may prefer to sell the business at the conclusion of the consolidation phase.

Alternatives

Asset stripping

One approach that has been widely used by bankers, many lawyers, trustees in bankruptcy and certain high profile executives involves slashing expenses and selling the maximum amount of assets as fast as possible in order to repay creditors. The goal is not to save the business; the goal is to save the bank and earn good fees and bonuses by doing so. Once the goal of repayment of lenders is achieved, the surviving managers must try to resuscitate the carcass and the real turnaround starts. It is easy to imagine that few companies survive the asset strippers.

The anorexia approach to health

The anorexia approach is to starve the business. This approach has been called other pejorative names: 'slash & burn', 'bayonet the wounded' and 'neutron bomb management' (destroy the people, leave the buildings). This approach is much like asset stripping, except the intention is to achieve short-term profitability. The typical methods include firing as many people as possible, especially research scientists, marketing analysts and others who do not contribute to immediate profits, stopping all capital expenditures except those that cannot be avoided by patching up the existing equipment and, possibly, using one of the forms of bankruptcy protection to wipe out the suppliers who in good faith supplied goods and services to the company.

This approach is fast and can be beneficial for the banks who get paid fast, beneficial for the lawyers and accountants who get well paid, and beneficial for the CEO who collects a fat bonus for restoring profitably. However, the approach can be very detrimental to the employees and to suppliers if a form of bankruptcy is used to wipe out all or a significant part of the monies owed them. The company may lose many good people and the goodwill of those remaining, it may lose the respect of its suppliers, its customers may be frightened away, and capital assets and the marketing and marketing processes may be neglected and become stale or even obsolete. Accordingly, the initial return to profitability may be illusionary – a dead cat bounce in the colorful economists' phrase.

What distinguishes the anorexia approach from the nuanced approach recommended in this book is near-total disregard for the medium to long-term health of the company; however, elements of this approach, such as proposals under the Bankruptcy Act or its variations, may be required in conjunction with more constructive efforts in order to restore a failing company to sustainable competitive vitality. Certainly, most turnarounds involve a strict diet to trim the corporate fat.

Slimming to the exit

A 'slimming to the exit' option may be implemented over one or more years. In this option, divisions and plants are closed or sold, product lines are phased out, and inventory, receivables and fixed assets are converted to cash. If all divisions are sold, the business is obviously closed. If one or a few divisions are retained, the nature of the original business is so extensively changed as to constitute the end of the old business and the creation of a new, much smaller business. Since 'slimming to the exit' implies a business with several divisions or units, this approach is not common among privately held companies.

Bet the company

This option is a desperate act of managerial panic or folly. High-risk bets may include an acquisition of a subsidiary or new technology, a major change in operations or marketing or a major capital expenditure that could strain an already strained balance sheet. These bets may either turnaround the company or accelerate its decline. There may be no middle ground. Betting the company may be doomed to failure if the acquisition, change or expenditure is targeted at only one of the company's issues and avoids interconnected issues or if there are inadequate managerial and financial resources to complete the change. An intangible factor is the congruence of culture of the acquirer and the acquired company. In an acquisition, incompatible corporate cultures can lead to expensive delays in melding operations and marketing. An acquisition by a company strong in the technology or marketing paradigm may require a rapid change in the acquired company to a much different corporate culture in terms of innovation, adaptability, incentives and rewards.

On the other hand, transformation may be reasonable

To paraphrase Sherlock Holmes, when all the other options are inadequate, a radical transformation by betting the company on an acquisition, new technology or a fundamental shift in operations and marketing may be one of the only two viable options. Of course, the remaining viable option would be to exit. Accordingly, a Turnaround CEO would not categorically rule out a 'bet the company' option; but the CEO would proceed with great caution in decision-making and careful implementation.

The last man standing: mergers of distressed companies

An infrequent option is the merger of two distressed companies to create a larger distressed company. Companies in a troubled or declining industry may merge so that the number of industry players declines as the industry contracts; in time a few players will dominate and may be able to realize oligopolistic profits. Obviously, a merger will not resolve serious flaws; however, the merged company may have sufficient volume to absorb overhead or achieve some economies of scale. For the merger of distressed companies to be successful there must be immediate elimination of duplication of staff and assets. This must be fast and thorough.

If The Turnaround Doesn't Turn

Some turnarounds fail. Others are terminated when the expectations of shareholders or lenders change or when compelling new information or economic conditions become known. In those cases, the companies move to the Exit position. The Turnaround CEO should be aware of the exit strategies so that they can be considered when and as required: sell the company, orderly liquidation and bankruptcy. Professional legal, accounting and bankruptcy advice is always required before making these decisions.

Sell the business

Normal business valuation approaches assume a sale to a buyer with no compelling reason to transact. Normal business valuation approaches may indicate that an Exit company has nominal or negative value: knowledgeable persons or corporations may not want to buy a company losing money or with an indefensible competitive position. Nonetheless, in special circumstances, Exit companies may be sold at premiums over the book value of equity to suppliers, customers or competitors, which may have a compelling reason to buy and which may pay a higher price than likely to be achieved through a bankruptcy or liquidation and at a lower transaction cost. Customers or suppliers may seek vertical integration. Competitors may wish to acquire production facilities, a distribution network or a customer base. It is important to know which potential buyers would benefit from acquiring the company's production facilities, trademarks, skilled work force and market position. The potential sale price may be calculated as a portion of the present value of the company's projected contribution margin over three to five years and as owned and managed by an industry player; the apportioned share of that notional value is allocated to the buyer and seller through the negotiation process. The drawbacks of a sell strategy are that there may be no buyers or it may take months to attract a buyer and consummate a transaction. Sale proceeds minus operating losses during the sale process may generate fewer funds for creditors and shareholders than an immediate shut down and liquidation.

Orderly liquidation

Orderly liquidation is the winding down of operations and the sale over a few months of all assets. An orderly liquidation avoids the haste and publicity of bankruptcy, and it has the potential to produce greater recoveries (than bankruptcy) for creditors and shareholders under certain conditions. Typically orderly liquidations make most sense if there are large investments in raw materials, work-in-progress inventories and finished goods or if the business has a seasonal peak sales period and the liquidation decision is made sufficiently in advance of the peak sales season to allow the maximization of the proceeds of converting inventories to accounts receivable to cash. In some circumstances advance notice of terminations (the so called working notice) may lessen severance costs. If demand for the assets weakens or if there are significant operating losses during the liquidation, an orderly liquidation may produce lesser recoveries (than bankruptcy). Company executives may conduct an orderly liquidation, either with legal and accounting guidance and creditor consent or under the direct monitoring or supervision of independent professionals appointed by creditors. Expert legal advice and a detailed budget covering the orderly liquidation are essential.

Bankruptcy

Bankruptcy is a formal and often expensive process defined by legislation whereby assets are sold and creditors are paid according to the creditors' legal rights, with the process being subject to court review and approval. Bankruptcy is subject to complex legislation and expert legal advice is essential. In addition, a bankruptcy will, usually, decrease net proceeds to the shareholders: potential buyers may offer to buy operating assets at a substantial discount and offer nominal amounts for trademarks, patents and other intangibles. On the other hand, if the nature of operations may expose the company, its officers and its directors to onerous risk, bankruptcy is advisable. Expert legal advice is essential.

Turnaround Essentials

The turnaround essentials are described in this chapter and a few will be more thoroughly discussed in later chapters.

Good Numbers

Turnaround companies usually have seriously flawed cost accounting systems and their financial statement numbers may be misleading. During a turnaround, tough and even irreversible decisions involving closing branches and selling divisions, dropping product lines, ending research projects and large scale layoffs may be made. These decisions are based, largely but not exclusively, on financial numbers. Good numbers are essential for good decisions. Verify that the numbers are at least approximately correct.

Accounting department

Modern business management needs good data. The accounting department is the single best-trained and equipped source of data - if it has senior management instructions and support. Accounting in a modern business is a staff function that – ideally - gathers, analyzes and reports financial and operational data in a managerially useful manner (and reports to shareholders and taxation authorities). Unfortunately, Turnaround and Exit companies often have weak accounting departments that produce inaccurate, inadequate and late information. The accounting department may have been starved of the financial and human resources required to develop and implement strong systems. Weak accounting is a symptom and cause of the Turnaround and Exit positions.

Ask the accounting department's customers (the marketing department, the factory and warehouse people and the company's bank) if they receive precise, useful, timely data. The feedback from these 'customers' will indicate the accounting department's contributions.

Financial statement accounting

Financial accounting is preparing financial statements and reports such as fixed asset and depreciation schedules and aged accounts receivable. Senior management should have a good intuitive sense of the accuracy of financial information. A strong indication of errant accounting is significant differences between the month-end financial statements for the eleventh month of the fiscal year and the auditor-approved year-end financial statements. Another indication of errant accounting is the existence of parallel or duplicate systems maintained by operations or marketing because they do not have confidence in the formal accounting system. If there are any misgivings about the accuracy of financial statement information, the company's auditors should be involved immediately.

Cost accounting

Cost accounting is ensuring that costs are allocated to products and activities so that senior management has the information to make sound decisions about products, customers, people and capital expenditures. Virtually every Turnaround company, and many other companies, have out-of-date or grossly wrong cost accounting. They do not know how much things really cost and, therefore, their decisions are either wrong or accidentally correct. The causes of faulty cost accounting may include accountants trained in financial accounting and not cost accounting, systems of cost allocation that were established several years previously and subsequently invalidated by changes in processes, and cost allocations based on nonsensical factors, ineptitude or negligence.

If there are misgivings about the cost accounting system or data, the planning process should proceed in two concurrent paths. Research and analysis of qualitative issues concerning personnel and management should proceed while an independent accountant or management consultant reviews the cost accounting system and its output. If the validity of data is confirmed, critical strategic decisions on products, customers, people and expenditures may be finalized. If the cost accounting data is flawed, the data should be corrected and the analysis of product and customer contribution margins should be done. Then, strategic decisions may be finalized.

The senior accountant

In larger companies undergoing a turnaround one of the early casualties is often the senior accountant. No experienced Turnaround CEO will want to tolerate the dangers of a senior accountant who is inadequate to the challenges. If the controller or Vice-President Finance has been in the job for more than five years, he or she may be stale; if training is refused or avoided, consider a change of personnel. There is another problem – uncommon, but occurring frequently enough to merit comment. A company accountant may come to believe that he or she knows best and may skew data or present data to the CEO or senior management in a manner to drive the accountant's preferred decisions. Deliberating withholding pertinent information or skewing or misrepresenting data merits dismissal.

Competitive Strength

A business must be good at something that customers value. The strength might be superior technology, consistent product quality or a high traffic location for a retailer. The strength does not have to be great. It just has to be something that customers value - a foundation to build on. If there is not a definable competitive strength, redefine the business to identify a cluster of attributes or characteristics which customers value or might value. If there is neither a current nor a potential competitive strength, the company is in the Exit Position.

Customer Goodwill

There must be customer goodwill, a base level of patronage and respect. This goodwill is shown by sales levels, sales trends and, most importantly, a hard-core base of customer loyalty. A striking example of customer goodwill is Apple Computer - a company that has an army of dedicated loyalists. Companies with strong customer loyalty and brand awareness are high potential candidates for successful turnarounds. Companies that have abused, consumed and dissipated customer goodwill may not be salvageable. Very satisfied customers can be advocates; passively indifferent customers are waiting to be poached by competitors. Brand values are what customers perceive and internalize, and later chapters will emphasize the importance of preserving and enhancing brand values and hence customer goodwill.

Creditor Co-Operation

Suppliers must continue to supply and bankers must refrain from demanding payment of loans. Owners of small and mid-sized businesses are naive beyond belief - they still believe that their banks are their friends. Makes a person wonder if those business owners still find Christmas presents from Santa Claus under the tree, dutifully wrapped by an aging mother or aunt. During the American and international credit contraction in 2008 commentators wrote and spoke of a 'flight to quality' as banks withdrew from high-risk exposures. For companies that means that if the banks don't think borrowers are quality, the banks take flight.

Typically, lenders and suppliers will have diminished confidence in management and an important part of the early stages of a turnaround is earning lenders' and suppliers' renewed confidence and trust. The reputation and track record of a newly hired Turnaround CEO or a Turnaround Consultant may help stabilize the banking relationship. They will advise the bank of the problems and the corrective measures being taken. A bank will co-operate if there is in the bank's opinion a reasonable expectation that the business will turn around and that the safety of the bank's advances will not deteriorate.

The bank may require a set of projected financial statements. Avoid hastily prepared financial projections that may be based on flawed assumptions. It is better to take a reasonable amount of time to prepare and provide an intelligent forecast. However, the practical reality is that the bank may not extend the luxury of time to provide the best forecast possible under tight deadlines; if so, the assumptions about internal and external factors should be thoroughly listed.

Suppliers are often not told of the problems, although invariably suppliers see the overdue accounts receivable, hear industry gossip and suspect the worst. Candid discussions with key suppliers should be considered, to gain and maintain co-operation (and supply) during the turnaround.

Communications

The most basic communication is telling people what they have to do in sufficient detail and clarity that they actually do it. Ideally, staff should understand the reasons for change and the urgency. Staff should be re-assured about the company's direction and prospects – to the extent that honest re-assurance can be given. But, communication does not assure that the message will be accepted or even believed. There are numerous examples of turnaround executives telling unionized labor that changes must be made to ensure a plant's survival, and having that communication rejected with the result that the particular plant was closed. Staff with five or ten or twenty years of seniority with a company have had five or ten or twenty years of hearing the old messages and the old thinking; it's unreasonable to expect that a twenty-minute speech will trump twenty years of indoctrination.

Shareholders, banks and major suppliers will require honest, forthright communication. Shareholders and bankers will have seen past failures to achieve promised improvements in corporate performance; it's unreasonable to expect that a two-hour meeting with shareholders or lenders will alleviate their legitimate concerns. The Turnaround CEO must deliver consistent communication and confirmation by performance. The Turnaround CEO will spend far more time in communication than in any other activity - at least half of his or her time will be communication of all sorts with all stakeholders.

Steady, unrelenting communication to answer stakeholder concerns

- What is the situation? What needs to be done?
- Why is change imperative?
- Why does a specific worker need to change?
- What will be the impact on the work environment and job security?
- Why should the bank continue to lend?
- Why should shareholders support or at least tolerate management's turnaround efforts?

Managerial Competency

Capable management that has made one or a few bad mistakes or been blindsided by rare events such as a natural disaster or political upheaval might complete a successful turnaround, with professional assistance. Commonly, the management team that led a company into a swamp cannot, unassisted, lead it out. Management, due to an excess of repentance or eagerness, may attempt an unassisted turnaround and the consequences can be unsatisfactory. Management may be blinded by historical viewpoints, may have psychological inhibitions against making tough decisions or be overwhelmed by the difficulties and complexities. Publicly traded companies may be more likely, than privately held companies, to fire the CEO who led the company into the swamp and to hire a new CEO with a turnaround mandate. The inclination may be to hire someone who has run a successful company but running a successful company requires somewhat different skills than leading a turnaround due to the uncertainties and the compression of time and the shortage of resources. Whether current management or newly hired management is charged with the responsibility of a turnaround, the board of directors and the shareholders should be conscious of the unique skills and attributes required, as discussed in a later chapter.

High Functioning Staff

Generally, turnaround companies have too many underperformers and too few good performers. Don't expect the people who were content to work for a company in a slow decline or a fast downward spiral to suddenly become gung-ho overachievers. There will be some hidden gems – high potential people who were beaten down by stifling managers, oppressive bureaucracy or dead-end strategy. The workhorses, laboring diligently and often underappreciated, may be energized by the new challenges and the new willingness to listen to their previously buried or suppressed ideas.

The world's greatest Turnaround CEO acting alone cannot turn around any business larger than a one-person barbershop; anything larger needs a high functioning staff. The Turnaround CEO must assess the senior and middle management of the company and the overall caliber of staff in the company. On a practical level the Turnaround CEO will focus on the senior executives or managers. Often one or two executives are clearly not going to be able to make the transition to the new, more demanding, faster paced environment. There is considerable cost in failing to deal decisively with underperformance in those executives' areas of responsibility. By means of rotation of staff out and new staff into the company and the inspiration and coaching of others, the Turnaround CEO must develop a high performing staff.

Prevention Of Calamities

Whether it's the perversity of fate or the revenge of the gremlins, the Turnaround CEO knows that nasty surprises happen and the CEO tries to minimize the frequency and nastiness of the surprises.

<u>Audits – financial, operational, environmental, and health & safety</u>

As repeatedly emphasized, turnarounds are messy, chaotic whirlwinds. The turnaround executive does not have the time, energy or expertise to verify that financial reporting, computer security, health & safety programs and quality standards are exemplary. Conversely, the turnaround executive cannot have armies of financial auditors, ISO auditors, health & safety consultants and industry-specific consultants swarming over staff and draining the budget. The practical, middle ground is to identify priorities for improvement or the potentials for catastrophic loss and then selectively commission audits by independent consultants who report directly to the Turnaround CEO. This process will contain expenditures while focusing remedial resources on the most important issues and will provide invaluable insight into the quality of the company's specialist staff.

Computer security

Computer security may be a risk with a small probability and a potentially disastrous consequence. It is a boring topic that executives ignore at their companies' peril. Security threats are not just from hackers and contaminated data. In privately held companies, the company controller or Vice President Finance may do double duty as the head of information technology; computer security is not a primary function but may be adequate for normal operations. What happens during a rapid transformation and possibly a downsizing during a turnaround? Some specialist personnel may be terminated, and they have the knowledge and may have the opportunity to do critical damage before their departure. The controller or Vice President Finance will be extremely busy and under intense pressure; lesser priorities will slip, inevitably.

A computer consulting firm should evaluate corporate vulnerability, design safeguards and monitor compliance. At an absolute minimum, companies should limit access to sensitive areas of their system to a small number of authorized personnel, make back-up copies daily and store the back-up copies off-premises. If need be, outsource computer security: there will be greater assurance of security and the controller or Vice President Finance will be freed to devote more time to generating accurate, useful and timely financial statements, cost accounting and reports on operational metrics.

Security

Companies undergoing a turnaround may quickly have fewer, disgruntled and overworked personnel and about the same amount of financial and physical assets to safeguard. In addition, the laxity of management that likely contributed to corporate underperformance likely extended to laxity of security. One option is to get some free consulting: ask the company's major insurers to assist in reviewing physical assets to determine best practices and to develop prioritized recommendations. Finally, keep your eyes open and your antennae up.

Fraud

Good numbers on the frequency and severity of fraud as a significant contributing factor to failing companies are not available; however, fraud happens often enough to merit vigilance. Managers and executives think fraud is relatively rare and certainly rare as a cause or significant cause of corporate failure; forensic accountants and other expert observers tend to believe that fraud is at least not uncommon. "According to research conducted by the Association of Certified Fraud Examiners (ACFE), U.S. organizations lose an estimated 7 percent of annual revenues to fraud."[6] If a large fraud is being committed, stopping the fraud may in itself achieve a turnaround.

While some frauds are cleverly hidden, other frauds are thinly disguised and the defrauding employee leaves potential clues such as deviations from standard administrative practices, odd working hours, deferred holidays and expensive lifestyles.

Classic formulation of who commits fraud

- Are trusted,
- Have the knowledge and opportunity, and
- Have a sense of being wronged in some way or being entitled in some way.

Detailed variance analysis of revenue and expenses can be helpful; but, the biggest, best help is just watching and being vigilant – always have the antennae up. If practical, the Turnaround CEO should sign all checks and approvals for electronic funds transfers.

---

[6] Association of Certified Fraud Examiners:
http://www.acfe.com/resources/publications.asp?copy=rttn

Questions to ask about payments

- Why did we spend this money?
- Who authorized it?
- What value did we receive?
- Can we go and look at what we bought?

Fraud may be detected by listening and meeting one-on-one with as many people as possible: inevitably there is the 'last honest person' in a company – someone who knows or suspects what's going on and would like to do the right thing. A confidential hot line for whistle-blowers should be considered. There is another way to stop some fraud: encourage ethical behavior and open communication. Ethical behavior sets the moral tone of the workplace and discourages the good employee from succumbing to temptation. Open communication is important.

The specialized search for fraud is called a forensic audit and is performed by specialized auditors. Forensic auditors should be engaged at the first suspicion of fraud and, subject to legal advice, before the suspected employee is questioned by management or dismissed. If there is no suspicion of fraud, there is merit in senior executives attending workshops on fraud and fraud prevention. There may be merit in a forensic review of corporate vulnerability to fraud.

<u>Insurance</u>

Turnaround companies cannot afford adequate insurance. Their shareholders, directors and officers cannot afford inadequate insurance. Insurable risks should be catalogued and where possible a program of risk mitigation should start. Qualified, independent professionals, not the company's staff or broker, should review insurance coverages on the basis of company risk and need. Directors and Officers insurance merit extra attention given the risks associated with a turnaround. The cost of insurance should be the last consideration. The trade-off between coverage and cost should be a board of directors decision.

Urgency

Urgency is one of the principles; as one of the essentials of a turnaround it might be better called 'extreme or intense urgency.' A point worth repeating: turnarounds differ from managing a company well by the compression of time and the scarcity of resources. Over lunch a veteran executive who had been involved in 44 corporate acquisitions in three years said that there was a six-week window after an acquisition to take control of the acquired company and to start to make changes; after six weeks complacency and passive resistance to the acquirer became pronounced. The window of change in a turnaround is short, too. Speed is essential. Get the facts. Make the best possible decisions on the available information. Implement fast. At all times, be vigilant; monitor the internal and external environment; and, be prepared to alter tactics in light of new information.

Board of Directors / Owner Support

Turnarounds are done by management, but management must have the mandate and the confidence and support of the board of directors or owners during the sometimes discouraging and sometimes harrowing crises that come with most turnarounds. When boards and owners make the fateful decision to turnaround a company, rather than to liquidate their investment, and when they select a Turnaround CEO, they must have the courage to be steadfast during the inevitable difficulties.

Legality & Ethics

Legal and ethical obligations should be scrupulously honored. The company's lawyer should brief the board of directors and senior management on directors' and officers' liabilities and creditors' rights. During the turnaround, the turnaround consultant and the company's lawyer should be consulted on every ambiguous situation.

In some cases, the pressures of a crisis have led people to make mistakes without thinking about their responsibilities. It can be tempting to avoid unpleasant honesty and it can be tempting and even it may seem essential to be dishonest at times. Don't do it. First, dishonesty only works until other people figure out that someone is a crook. Second, if you have lived an honest, reputable life to this point, don't sacrifice your dignity and self-worth. Third, in the longer term, your life will be better if you are ethical. It takes guts and courage and sometimes steel-edged nerves, but ethical behavior is the better way.

Turnaround Phases

Turnarounds happen in different industries and with different severity of internal problems, cash flows, external environment, core issues that caused or contributed to the deterioration, and human and financial resources available. That's over 2,400 different combinations of factors. Therefore, not one roadmap will suffice for all turnarounds and not one chronology will be appropriate. The following description of turnaround phases presents a logical, natural progression of ideas and actions for ease of writing and reading. It may also give a false impression of exactitude. The reality is that turnarounds only more-or-less follow these phases and may have meanderings, doublings back and jumps forward. The Turnaround CEO must stay fluid to respond effectively to new information.

Conservation Of Working Capital

Cash budgeting & management

In a turnaround, the corporate resources are usually declining at an alarming rate. Immediately, within the first two or three days, a rolling six-week cash budget should be prepared. It should show weekly or, in some cases, daily projected cash receipts and cash disbursements. The actual cash balances should be compared to budget and the budget should be updated weekly – for example, every Friday morning. It is important to track the previous forecasts and to compare those forecasts to actual cash balances; this will help identify any biases in the cash budget. The first several cash budgets may be flawed but within a few weeks the controller should be able to refine the cash budget into a useful planning and control tool.

The controller will normally confer with the Turnaround CEO on the cash policy – what amount to keep in reserve, what payables will be paid in priority to less important payables, and what discounts to offer to accelerate accounts receivable collections. Then the CEO and the controller can meet weekly to consider the company's current and projected cash position. In some cases the senior sales and production executives should be involved as their projections of sales and expenses will affect the cash budget. The weekly meetings will typically end with an agreed amount, called the Open To Pay amount; the controller will then issue payments equal to that amount. Usually, the Turnaround CEO will not have the time or desire to select specific accounts to pay; once the policy is set and once the rolling cash budget is agreed to, the controller will be authorized to implement the cash policy.

Stop the burn rate

In the surreal world of dotcoms in the late 1990s, executives spoke of their 'burn rate' – how fast they were spending the money they had raised from credulous investors. Turnarounds are the opposite.

Cash conservation measures

- Delay payables, if not already stretched.
- Meet with key suppliers to negotiate extensions of terms or discounts.
- Settle older or disputed accounts receivable, possibly at a discount.
- Consult with labor lawyers and implement lay-offs or reduced hours / week.
- Implement a 30 or 90 day moratorium on capital expenditures.
- Ask 'do we need to spend this money?' on every expenditure – grass cutting to Christmas decorations to travel expenses – not everything should be cut, but everything must be critically evaluated: expenses are cancelled, continued or postponed for later evaluation.
- Sell surplus assets and all old or obsolete inventories, at a discount in most cases.

Stop the bleeding

In first aid, a priority is 'stop the bleeding'. In turnarounds, a priority is 'stop the bleeding'. Stopping the bleeding is more than just conserving cash. Stopping the bleeding is stopping unprofitable or unproductive activities. Deep cuts early save cash and inspire lenders and shareholders that management knows the problems and has the guts to tackle the problems. Conversely, there should be a balance between the short-term imperatives and preservation of core resources essential to recovery and growth. The cost structure must be re-examined – thoroughly. Few companies with more than two products and two customers know their costs. Getting to really, really understand the costs and the cost drivers may take months, so the process must start almost immediately. Plants or divisions may be closed if they are so bad that the odor of their poor performance affects the rest of the company. It is usually better to at least consider stopping entire divisions or departments or activities rather than trying to squeeze a little here and there. Be wary of assurances that a division or a truck route or a product line 'just needs more time to recover'. Set tough targets, such as 'fix this in 90 days or close it', and enforce the targets.

Cash & creditors

Negotiations with the bank and major creditors may begin immediately. The first step is often restoring a basic level of trust and confidence that management is attentive, hard working and straightforward in its communications. It is worthwhile to re-read the section on creditor cooperation.

Control Of Expenses

Control of Expenses is different than Conservation of Working Capital. Conservation of Working Capital is surgery with an axe. Control of Expenses is not brutal in the same degree; Control of Expenses is the application of judicious managerial judgment of all expenses on the basis of value for money and congruence between the expenditure and the mid- to long-term strategy. Evaluate expenses on the basis of their short-term contribution to profits and their relevance to mid-term recovery. Some employees may be laid off, warehouses may be consolidated and certain marketing programs may be curtailed or canceled. Decisions should balance the need to conserve cash with the need to preserve competitive strengths. Improved expense productivity starts with good metrics. There should be monthly or weekly tracking and reporting of key expense productivity metrics, such as sales and gross margins, sales and tonnage per mile or kilometer, overtime wages as a per cent of total wages, total wages as a per cent of sales and so on. If it's not measured, it's not managed.

Asset productivity

It is fairly common to find 'lazy' assets – assets that are not adequately hard working and productive. Of course, no assets are really 'lazy' assets; there are only assets that management has underutilized. Squeezing extra productivity from each asset class will decrease the need for external funding and may reduce the need for capital expenditures. Improved asset productivity starts with good metrics. There should be monthly or weekly tracking and reporting of key asset productivity metrics, such as inventory turnover rates, accounts receivable collection rates, miles or kilometers per truck, tonnage per grain elevator and so on. Again, if it's not measured, it's not managed.

The common example is inventory turnover rates; increasing the inventory turnover rate will decrease the investment in inventory and in warehouse space. Another example: the entrenched managers of a distribution company claimed that the company had barely enough trucks – working about an average of 40 hours / week. The Turnaround CEO forced a small reduction in the number of trucks, which forced better scheduling; the Turnaround CEO then forced a further small reduction in the number of trucks, which forced even better scheduling. In other words, at times it may be better to reduce the assets first and figure out how to do the deliveries later. Necessity may be the mother of improved management.

Consolidation Of Progress

After the easy and the urgent tasks are done, start over. At this point, the company should be at breakeven, or better. Expenses have to be re-examined to identify additional savings. Cash from asset reductions should normally be used to reduce debt. Cash flow from operations should normally be used to increase marketing of profitable products. The financial status should be stabilized although likely at a level below prosperity. A new phase starts. This is the start of re-building sustainable competitive vitality. The strategic vision that was seen vaguely through the smoke and fog of the early weeks and months while stopping the bleeding and controlling expenses should become a clearer, articulated strategy. Turnaround companies usually have operational and marketing problems that are both symptom and cause of the turnaround. Some of the problems may require months or years to fix; at this point the emphasis should be on fixing those problems. The Consolidation of Progress phase is about preparing for recovery and growth and it will include repairing morale, expanding profitable product lines, possibly some market re-positioning or product re-engineering, and probably some financial re-engineering involving long term financing, equity injections or debt to equity swaps by suppliers. The phase may last two or more years, and will not be completed until the business achieves sustainable competitive vitality.

Continuation Or Sale

Once the company is stabilized at or about breakeven, a decision should be made either to move into a recovery and growth mode of a successful turnaround or to sell the business. Because recovery and growth are arduous and lengthy and present new, uncertain risks, shareholders may prefer to sell the business at the conclusion of the consolidation phase. A decision to sell before the company achieves the benefits of recovery and growth may be a rational decision. The success of the early phases of the turnaround will have increased the value of the business, perhaps substantially; continued ownership during the Consolidation of Progress phase when the company seeks to achieve recovery and growth exposes the shareholders to new risks and may require a change in leadership. It is entirely understandable for shareholders to sell, reaping gains in value to that point while avoiding the risk to their equity of a failure during the Consolidation of Progress phase. Conversely, selling at any time means that shareholders lose potential future capital appreciation of the company.

CASE STUDY: KNITTED LADIES' WEAR [7]

The Company

The company was a manufacturer of knitted lady's clothing. It was located in modest premises in Toronto. Equipment, although not state of art, was adequate and reasonably well maintained. In the previous three years losses ranged from $60,000 to $175,000. Sales in each of the previous two years were $4,000,000.

Bank indebtedness was $800,000 and the company was deficient in all of its covenants. The bank transferred the account to "Special Loans" and froze the lending at its current level. The bank demanded an action plan within 30 days. The bank also recommended that the company engage a consultant to work with the owners to develop an action plan to turnaround the company.

Illustration: Alexandra Astafyeva

The Action Plan

Working with the two owners, the consultant performed a complete review of all aspects of the operations and presented an action plan to the bank, along with cash flow and profit projections. The owners' had a total commitment to the survival of the company

---

and they maintained the discipline required to stay with the action plan and to make appropriate alterations as circumstances indicated. The consultant was able to demonstrate to the bank that the shareholder / managerial commitment was there and that the goals were both reasonable and achievable. After extensive discussions, the bank accepted the action plan. With the cooperation of the bank and the discipline and diligence of the owners, a successful turnaround was achieved. The following summarizes the major actions taken over 24 months and the results.

Accounts Receivable, Re-pricing & Customer Retention, Accounts Payable

- A review of each customer was undertaken to determine profitability, payment history and products purchased.
- Approximately 30 customers were dropped as they were not profitable or were not willing to adhere to payment terms.
- Old and slow paying accounts receivable were resolved either by offering discounts for fast payment, or by turning these accounts over for collection.
- Price increases were instituted over a period of six months on the most popular product lines.
- Major creditors were approached and arrangements were made to extend existing balances over a 12-24 month period, on condition that all current amounts would be paid according to new terms.

Manufacturing, Products & Inventories

- A new plant foreman was hired with more experience than the previous foreman.
- The number of products manufactured was reduced from 37 to 26.
- Slow moving and redundant stock was liquidated through a jobber.
- Inventory was counted monthly and reconciled to the book records.
- As the number of products manufactured was reduced, the cost of material decreased because larger quantities of fewer products were purchased at lower prices.
- Terms with suppliers were arranged that included either discounts for early payment or extended terms for bulk purchases.

Labor Costs

- The number of employees was appropriate for the volume produced; however, overtime hours, which had become a common occurrence, were eliminated by creating a second shift when required.

Management and Administration

- The two owners agreed to assume clearly defined responsibilities, with one dealing with production and the other dealing with sales, marketing and general administration.
- Management salaries were reduced by 40% in the first year and 25% in the second year.
- The existing office manager/accountant was replaced.
- All computer systems were reviewed and enhancements were made to both the accounting and production systems.
- Accurate monthly financial statements were completed by the tenth day of the month.
- A new lease was negotiated with the landlord for seven years, which included a reduced rent for the first two years and a higher rent for the remaining five years of the lease.

Results After 24 Months

- After an initial decrease, sales returned to $4,000,000, and gross profit increased by 6-8%.
- Accounts receivable collections decreased from 70-95 days to 50-60 days.
- Inventory decreased by $175,000.
- After 12 months the company lost $25,000 and in the second year earned $160,000.

Commentary on the case study

The accountants' paradigm dominated this turnaround – with very good results. Profits averaged about ($110,000) in the three years before the turnaround. In the second year of the turnaround profits were $160,000. This was an improvement of about $270,000 on sales of $4,000,000, or 6.75% of sales. It appears that bank loans decreased from $800,000 to about $200,000 (based on the decreases in accounts receivable and inventories and the two-year profits, and assuming depreciation covered capital expenditures).

Another interesting point is that the bank – not the owner–managers – identified the crisis of underperformance and pushed for remedial action. The fact that the bank recommended a consultant is a strong indication that the bank had concerns about the ability of management and maybe about the credibility of management. Implicit in the case study is the role of the turnaround consultant in communicating with the bank; obviously, the company is the consultant's client and the consultant's loyalty must be to the client. However, a consultant has a higher duty of loyalty – a duty of loyalty to his or her professional integrity. One can assume that the consultant's reputation helped persuade the bank to be cooperative. Every communication should be pre-approved by the client, either in concept or, ideally, in written detail. During turnarounds, meetings with the bank should generally be three-way: company, consultant and bank; this maintains transparent communication.

In every turnaround the owner-managers talk a good story; they say that they are committed to a turnaround. Banks have heard those assurances many, many times. In this case, the owner-managers took a substantial reduction in remuneration, which may well have been more reassuring to the bank than the usual bland, verbal assurances.

A turnaround is a process to restore a failing company to sustainable competitive vitality; however, the company at the point covered by this case study may not have achieved a sustainable competitive vitality. The case does not provide enough information to confirm if management had experienced a fundamental awakening or if management would revert to its apparently lethargic ways once the financial and bank pressures diminish. A highly experienced risk manger in a major bank said once that companies that were in trouble during one recession and survived had a very high probability of being in trouble during the next recession. This company has a high probability of experiencing a second crisis if the owner-managers have not permanently raised the quality of their management. In addition to the question of management, it is reasonable to wonder about the microeconomic environment. The company is in the garment industry in a high wage country. There are other factors that may affect the company's competitiveness, such as the advantage of proximity to North American customers, shortened shipping and order fulfillment cycles and economic use of technology to diminish labor content. It may be difficult for the company to enjoy competitive vitality if it does not invest in operational and supply chain efficiencies.

Overall, it would appear that this turnaround – to the point in time covered by the case study – was really a partial turnaround; the Conservation of Working Capital and the Control of Expenses was admirably done; however, the Consolidation of Progress phase must still be traversed before one could consider this to be a complete, successful turnaround.

CHAPTER 4: TURKEYS DON'T FLY: GET THE RIGHT PEOPLE

It is rare to find a company that has deteriorated to the point that it is in a turnaround position and yet has a cadre of excellent, dedicated people. Virtually every seasoned turnaround specialist has said the same thing: "Sometimes I did not make personnel changes fast enough."

On a Monday morning in February 1983 a small financial institution terminated 28% of its staff; a vice-president explained to the surviving staff 'Better some of us go now than all of us go later.' [8] Good point!

Never-ending questions about personnel

- What is the best organization chart for this company for now and for next year? Do we have the right managerial and staff positions? Do we have the right people in the right positions? How do we align our people with our strategy?
- Can staff, with training and motivation, successfully implement the strategic choices that, at this point, appear most promising for the company? Can certain people grow into high performers within 90 days or 6 months?
- Can this management team, with training and motivation, successfully implement the strategic choices that, at this point, appear most promising for the company?
- If not, what are the detailed plans to upgrade or replace staff? At what cost? What are the detailed plans to upgrade or replace members of the management team? At what cost?
- What skills must this company retain or enhance in order to restore sustainable competitiveness? Who has special skills? How do we retain them?
- Who has the 'will to win'? Can they grow the will to win?

---

[8] Names withheld for reasons of confidentiality.

Turnaround companies cannot afford to warehouse deadwood. Companies should make a reasonable, intelligent effort to match surplus people with corporate priorities but priorities should not be set to match or absorb weak people. Contract employees and part-time employees are usually first to be terminated. Serious underperformers are often obvious and well known; they should go fast and their departures will raise the average staff quality. Then, the hard choices start. Generally, it is appropriate to fire someone who has not shown satisfactory improvement after receiving the benefit of every reasonable effort to train, develop, coach and motivate within the time constraints of a turnaround, or if it is not practical to shift the person to alternate work important to the company. Consider making computer back-ups, having a locksmith change all locks and hiring a security guard if there are any potential dangers or risks to the company or its staff. But, do not procrastinate.

Legal Minefield: Hire A Labor Lawyer

Within the first week or two weeks, the Turnaround CEO should select his or her labor lawyer. The labor lawyer may be the company's current lawyer, or a new labor lawyer may be retained. Make the arrangements promptly as the need for expert legal guidance will come sooner rather than later. Subject to wide variations due to each company's situation, expect that legal costs over 18 – 24 months will be 0.5% of annual sales. This money is well spent as it will save money on later lawsuits and labor board hearings and the drain on management time fighting legal challenges. If there is any doubt about an employee issue, check with a labor lawyer.

Severances & A Budget For Severances

Within the first two weeks, establish a budget for severance costs during the next two years. The budget will be an estimate, but at least it will be an attempt to quantify the probable costs of one aspect of a turnaround. The costs will vary with labor laws, the total number of employees, the seniority of employees, the provisions in any union contracts, whether plant closures or downsizings are anticipated, and the total salaries and wages expense. So, subject to wide variations, a Turnaround CEO might budget on severance costs of 10% - 30% of total salaries and wages in each of the first two years, with those amounts adjusted for the specifics of the situation.

How big will the personnel disruption be? It depends on the severity of the corporate sickness. It is reasonable to expect personnel rotation of 15% to 75% over three years, with most being in the 6 to 18 month period. Expect 15% rotation if the revenues and needs justify stable employment numbers and if there appears to be only a few people who are unsuitable for their roles. Expect 75% rotation if revenues and needs mandate reductions in employment numbers and if many managers and staff are unsuitable for their roles. Surprisingly, high rotation of staff happens in the non-business sector, too: recently a school principal said that she had been assigned by her school board to do a turnaround of a middle school; in three years she had a 75% rotation of teachers and custodial staff, achieved through early retirements and transfers.

Turnaround companies usually do not have the cash to pay severances and yet do not have the cash to pay unproductive people to stay. The dilemma is resolved by paying severances over time rather than in single large amounts. The monthly cost is about the same as keeping the people, but at least there is an end. A disadvantage is that accounting principles require expensing of the total severance in that fiscal quarter or year, rather than accrual and monthly expensing; this accounting treatment will worsen losses but not cash flow and it can be explained to lenders and shareholders.

The Uncooperative & obstructionist

Turnarounds involve change, sometimes wrenching change. There may be a repudiation of the former, comfortable psychological workplace contract and the imposition of a new psychological contract; this will be stressful for most people. Some people will not be able to adjust or simply refuse to adjust. A few will be obstructionist. Uncooperative and even obstructionist staff and managers believe that they are doing a good job. They see no reason to change, they may not believe that the Turnaround CEO, especially if he is from outside the company, knows anything that they should learn, and they may even conspire to undermine the Turnaround CEO. Personal loyalty is not required and each person is entitled to his or her own perspective, but vipers must be dealt with. The Turnaround CEO must be vigilant and he or she must confront uncooperative behavior and every effort should be made to get uncooperative managers to amend their behaviors and attitudes. Those who do not respond constructively within weeks or a few months (maximum) should be terminated. It is impossible to complete a turnaround with bad attitude managers. It is impossible within the compression of time that characterizes a turnaround to re-energize people with a deeply ingrained attitude of mediocrity or entitlement.

Remuneration Of Shareholders, Managers & Staff

Within the first month, assess the reasonableness of compensation. Generally, rank and file staff and hourly workers are paid at or close to market wages and there is little injustice and little opportunity to adjust individual remuneration (although there may be opportunities to adjust the number of staff and hence the total wage cost). The cost of management is almost always the more immediate issue; in fact, the cost of a recently hired Turnaround CEO may mean that adjustments to the total cost of management become urgent.

<u>Non-shareholder-managers</u>

Assessing the reasonableness of the remuneration of non-shareholder / managers is straightforward. There are surveys published by leading human resource consulting firms and industry associations that outline industry standards to guide the salary negotiation between the company and the non-shareholder manager.

<u>Shareholder-managers</u>

The reasonableness of the remuneration of shareholder / managers is more difficult to assess and may be a point of serious contention with other shareholders and lenders if the amount of shareholder / manager remuneration appears to be based on personal consumption expectations. One witty observer has stated that a certain owner- manager was engaged in 'on the job consumption of wealth'. If, as is the case in some turnaround situations, managerial consumption has not been constrained by the company's ability to pay or by prohibitions in banking agreements, then changes must be made promptly. If remuneration is more than is justified, the solvency of the company may be jeopardized and relationships with other shareholders may become strained. Also, there is an unrecorded and unintended transfer of wealth from inactive shareholders and lenders to the overpaid shareholder / manager. The Turnaround CEO must stop all perks and benefits that are not justified by current contributions to the company. If remuneration is less than justified – a rarity - there has been a subsidy of the company by the underpaid shareholder / manager, and the company's performance is worse than the financial statements indicate. The Turnaround CEO will most likely have little financial resources to correct any underpayment to shareholder / managers. An equitable approach is set shareholder / manager remuneration based on the lower of the company's ability to pay and the total of the theoretical components of remuneration.

The theoretical components of remuneration

- Return On Labor: The shareholder / manager is entitled to a salary and benefits, reflecting the skills and achievements of the job, like any other employee.
- Return On Investment: The shareholder / manager is entitled to receive dividends, redemptions of shares and distribution of cash proportionate to shares owned.
- Return On Money Lent: Shareholder loans are legitimate debts. Principal payments and interest comparable to rates payable to other lenders should not be included in remuneration. However, covenants in agreements with lenders may limit payments on shareholder loans.
- Other Payments: Non-standard payments such as bonuses, perks and loans to shareholder / managers are sometimes made.

Staff

During the early stages of a turnaround, there will be no money and little time to adjust remuneration; however, the minimum remuneration goal must be to pay best those who contribute most. Some jobs can be rated by results and the workers can be paid for results. Many jobs involve co-operation and inter-dependency; therefore, group, divisional and even company-wide incentive programs and profit sharing may be more equitable than individual incentives. Rewards should recognize diverse contributions and encourage co-operation appropriate to the company's objectives. Avoid reward systems that deliberately or accidentally create many losers and few winners. Avoid annual raises which only drive up payroll costs; instead, pay bonuses for special contributions, although payments of bonuses may increase subsequent severance obligations.

Highly Paid & Key People

All the people in the company are important but some are more important than others. In the first few weeks start to identify those who are needed for the turnaround. Take inventory of the company's managers and staff, with special attention to highly paid and key people. Assess each person's current and potential contribution and identify gaps between contributions and corporate requirements. Delegate to the senior HR person the preparation of a simple matrix analysis. It should list every employee, his / her wage or salary rate plus employee benefits, actual earnings and benefits in the previous year, number of years with the company, and estimated high and low range of market wage or salary plus benefits. The total of historical earnings must equal historical wage, salary and benefits according to the financial statements. In smaller, privately held companies the salaries of the most senior executives may be withheld, except from the CEO and HR manager and controller, for reasons of confidentiality. The Turnaround CEO and a few trusted senior managers should review the matrix of personnel. They should list each person's key skills and rank their ability and willingness to make significant contributions over the next twelve months.

The definition of key person is: there would be a significant disruption if the person died, was incapacitated or quit. Include any occupational group, such as polymer scientists or tool and die makers, that is crucial to corporate success. This list will be invaluable in identifying those who should be terminated, those who should be retained and any cases of excessive and insufficient compensation. Conversely, few businesses employ people of rare skills. Generally, employees have important but identifiable skills that are replaceable (with training) in the labor market. A less obvious point is that employees do not make a sacrifice of previously acquired skills if they are retrained. Still less obvious are the observations that employees often have company-specific and industry-specific skills, customer and product knowledge and familiarity with the corporate culture. Their skills, knowledge and familiarity are what make employees valuable - if there is congruence with the external environment and corporate strategy. A company cannot build excellence with employee skills that are inadequate for the task of delivering or creating excellence.

Management

Do not procrastinate on dealing with managers. The bottleneck of a bottle is at the top; in companies, too. The rotation in the managerial ranks may need to be phased – with the most serious issues dealt with in the first three months and weak and marginal performers dealt with in the 6 to 18 month period. There may even be a third wave of personnel changes; after 18 – 24 months it will be clear which managers hired to replace the previous managers are ineffective. Rotation in the managerial ranks may be in the 50% - 75% range. The management of companies that are in a turnaround due to external shocks such as a sudden regulatory or economic change may be quite good. In other cases, management may be deficient: lazy, complacent, incompetent and self-satisfied. In between there is the majority of management of failing businesses: sincere, overwhelmed, out of ideas, dispirited and disillusioned. Amazingly, almost all Turnaround (and Exit) companies have a common characteristic (in addition to not knowing their costs): their shareholder / managers and managers do not work hard enough. Quality of management is determined by knowledge (scientific, technological or business), skills (inter-personal skills, group dynamics), characteristics (detail orientation, ethics, integrity) and the application of the knowledge, skills and characteristics appropriate to the company and its industry and challenges. No single management style is appropriate to every industry. Managing a chain of muffler shops is different than managing a resort hotel: the customers, product, people and assets are different.

A simple way to estimate the right number of managers is to visualize deducting one manager, and then another and another, until there is a barely perceptible decrease in corporate effectiveness; then add back one manager: that is the right number. Another equally unscientific method is to compare the five-year trend in profits and the five-year trend in the ratio of managers to total employees. A third method, best saved for the late stages of a turnaround when growth plans are being developed, is estimating how much the company could grow without adding any managers. If the company could grow 0% - 10%, it probably is understaffed with managers. If it could grow 10% -20%, there are probably sufficient managers to ensure control and continuity. If it could grow 20% or more, there may be excessive management.

Middle management is a common target for downsizing; however, middle management provides continuity of institutional experience and wisdom, facilitates smooth implementation of standard operating policies, guides junior staff who may lack experience in either the company or the marketplace and is the source of future corporate leadership. These are people who will contribute to the Consolidation of Progress phase. So, terminations of middle managers should be judicious.

CFO / Controller & HR Manager

The Chief Financial Officer or controller in smaller companies and the HR manager are key positions. It is imperative that these positions be staffed with professionals who have the skills, diligence and integrity to be trusted advisers and reliable implementers. There have been situations where untrustworthy people in those positions have misled the Turnaround CEO and damaged the turnaround process. The experienced Turnaround CEO will watch these two positions very closely in the first three months until unreserved confidence can be placed in the individuals. If unreserved confidence cannot be placed in them, terminate them as soon as possible.

Measure Performance & Do Appraisals

Decisions affecting the company's people must be consistent with ethics, labor laws and common sense. Nonetheless, Turnaround companies have considerable scope for improvements in attitudes and policies that specifically support corporate goals. Goals need to be specific and results need to be measured. Performance improvement without measurement is unlikely. The Turnaround CEO will not have the time to do personnel appraisals; however, not doing personnel appraisals saves time in the near-term but will cost much more time and money when underperformers are terminated. Also, doing performance appraisals forces the Turnaround CEO to think through personnel issues and to confront problem personnel. So, get the appraisals done and done thoroughly.

Hiring & Training

A hiring decision is a spending decision, just as a capital expenditure decision is a spending decision. Some companies make hiring decisions quickly, with little real thought about long term needs, often not thoroughly checking references, not using an industrial psychologist's testing service and with no planning of the post-hiring training, orientation and guidance, either through mentoring or a 'buddy system.' Then, companies wonder why they have a bunch of duds. It's not the employees' fault. An excellent manager in a Go For Gold company may not adapt to a new position with a turnaround company. Some of the people who are hired early in the turnaround process may not be successful due to a bad hiring decision or an evolution in the company's needs. Be prepared to do a second round of terminations and hiring after 12 – 24 months.

Training and especially cross-training may be neglected or even stopped during a turnaround. This saves money in the short-term but hampers the flexibility to make future changes in personnel and limits the potential to grow in the late stage of a successful turnaround. Accordingly, in the earliest stage of a turnaround, training may be suspended, except in health & safety and regulatory compliance. Use the time and money saved to develop an economical training plan consistent with the company's priorities for the following 6 – 18 months.

Organization & Culture

The Turnaround CEO may inherit a chaotic (rhymes with idiotic) organizational structure that may be flawed under normal circumstances and ineffective for a turnaround: people may have multiple bosses who give conflicting orders. Managers may have little authority and a justifiable fear of making decisions. Chaotic organizations produce weak financial results, weak managers and dispirited staff. The Turnaround CEO may need to make a near-immediate adjustment to the organization chart and one or more adjustments as the turnaround progresses and the company's needs and available personnel change. During the early months of a turnaround the organization will likely be highly centralized. The centralized model is not what management consultants and academics recommend for most companies in most situations; however, the Turnaround CEO must be deeply involved in all aspects of the company until he or she knows what all the key problems are and the capabilities of senior managers. The disadvantages are a crushing CEO workload and a limitation on the contributions of other personnel. By the Consolidation of Progress phase the Turnaround CEO should work towards optimizing the organization. The organization should be designed to meet the company's high priority objectives, not to avoid the unpleasantness of a demotion or outplacement and not to legitimize historical practice. Focus resolutely on the company's current and future high priorities.

Company culture is the attitudes, values and ingrained behavior that shape and guide how well people work and, like a societal culture, it is the product of evolutionary changes over many years. A strong company culture binds people together, gives a shared vision and facilitates communication. On the other hand, a strong culture may blind people to changes in the external environment and lead to active or passive obstruction of revitalization and transformation. Unfortunately, the cultures of turnaround companies may be inconsistent with the new imperatives of well-defined corporate objectives. Revitalizing an entire organization may take more than a year even with the harsh push of a desperate crisis. Change may mean breaking some implicit psychological contracts between the company and its employees and between employees as to what constitutes good behavior and the associated rewards. It is preferable that the breaking of psychological contracts be by mutual consent and with much notice and preparation. Explain the need for change and the benefits, and explain again and again. Change the subjective reality (how people perceive the company, its industry, its relationships with customers and suppliers and their personal roles) by steady, unremitting re-enforcement. Management must live the new truths.

CASE STUDY: TIRE RECYCLING[9]

-
- **Illustration: Alexandra Astafyeva**

- The Company
- The company started as a family owned and operated tire recycling business. Later it was sold to a major US auto-parts manufacturer and the founder's two sons continued with the company. In 1990 the sons of the founder and a Canadian based venture capital fund bought the company in a highly leveraged buyout. One of the sons became CEO and the other son became Senior Vice President.

The venture capital fund was publicly traded although the rubber recycling company was not. The venture capital fund saw an opportunity to change the perception of the recycling company to a "green" company thereby increasing its notional valuation. A higher notional valuation of the company would, it was expected, cause a higher stock market valuation of the venture capital fund. Under the new ownership and management the company was highly leveraged and it incurred a substantial loss. The company was not able to support the lifestyles of the two sons or meet the aspirations of the venture capital fund. The company hired a turnaround consultant on a year-long contract. He

---

[9] © J. Keith Robson, 2008

concluded that the company must reduce manufacturing costs, and improve the quality of the product and the dismal safety record of the plant.

The Products

The main products were a variety of shields controlling airflow or insulating heat from entering the passenger space of passenger cars. These products were mainly pressed items or stamped from flat sheet. In addition there were some more highly engineered injection molded components that were made from compound materials. The passenger car products were almost totally sold to Ford, Chrysler and GM. About 20% of the revenue was floor mats and molded beds for pickup trucks and mud flaps for trucks. These products were cheap and effective for commercial applications but not the high quality that the consumer market demanded. Several new non-automotive products were under development such as pads for railroad crossings and surrounds for sewer access covers. A minor revenue source was the sale of shredded steel from the tires as scrap to electric furnace steel plants. Another minor revenue source was government grants derived from the tax on new tires. Recovered nylon was disposed at a loss.

The Raw Materials

The primary raw materials were recycled rubber and new un-vulcanized rubber. Recycled rubber was from shredding used tires. New un-vulcanized rubber was waste from making new tires. Un-vulcanized rubber was used to bind or tie together the shredded rubber. At that time it was not possible to de-vulcanize rubber. The business was dependent on supplies of used tires and supplies of waste material from tire manufacturers. In the prior years the company had had some difficulty buying the waste tire material as tire manufacturing in North America was declining and other companies were competing for the waste rubber. The company had adopted a strategy of bidding for every piece of material. The result was that the cost of raw material and the investment in raw material inventory went up, which used scarce cash. Also, rising rubber costs artificially inflated the value of the raw material inventory creating accounting profit that disguised the real cash flow.

A large part of the rubber inventory was stored outside because of a shortage of warehouse space. Sometimes outside storage ruined the rubber due to the amount of cured (sun-baked) rubber and foreign objects that had been collected in the material. It was often necessary to mix the rubber that had been stored outside with newly acquired rubber. The variable quality of raw material reduced productivity and increased rejects, and the company missed delivery times to customers. Meanwhile, the major automotive customers were rapidly moving to just-in-time delivery. The result was material that was expensive, sometimes damaged by the sun, unpredictable in quality and expensive to process.

Production Management & Labor

There was very little professional manufacturing management and supervision was based on a few tough supervisors often leading shifts of people predominantly of their own ethnic origin. The workplace was unpleasant due to the heat and smell from the heated rubber. The company relied on low cost immigrant labor consisting of five language groups. Many workers had very limited English language skills. One or two ethnic groups dominated each shift. A supervisor from the major ethnic group and unofficial leaders of the other ethnic groups led the workers on each shift and provided translation as required. Communication between the five major ethnic groups was limited and depended upon the unofficial leaders of each group. Workers were relatively uneducated but they did have skills learnt on the job.

Health & Safety

The machinery was generally very big, powerful and hot. Grinding machinery often jammed. Accidents happened regularly, even with proper machinery guards installed. This situation was made even more difficult to resolve by all the different languages and cultural factors in the workplace. The employees were terrified of losing their jobs and often broke the rules to attempt to keep up with demands of the supervisors. The supervisors pushed production at almost any risk to health & safety, but they still failed to achieve the required output.

Remedial Actions

Production Management & Labor

The company hired an experienced manufacturing director and two bright young engineering graduates, one of whom stayed with the company for many years. The company hired an experienced HR manager who could help with the creation of an incentive program and communicate with the employees in some of the five different languages. The very capable maintenance manager who had been working in very difficult circumstances developed and put in place new preventative maintenance procedures. By the end of the year a new engineering director had been added to the team and the development of new products was accelerated.

A group of industrial engineering consultants who had worked previously with the consultant was contracted to streamline the manufacturing process. This involved all the supervisors and in-house engineering and maintenance staff as well as some of the key individuals who were the leaders in their ethnic communities. The whole manufacturing process was mapped from start to finish, the bottlenecks identified and unnecessary operations identified. Then, teams of people set about identifying solutions to specific issues.

In one case a key machine was a critical bottleneck and the supervisors and staff could not see any way of improving the output even though there appeared to be considerable idle machine time. After the consultants had spent hours watching the process and timing the various actions it became clear that theoretically the machine had almost double the capacity but it needed a complete rethink of the loading of raw materials. The supervisor was very cooperative and workers were keen to test new approaches. All went well initially but once the consultants had moved on, staff began slipping back into the old way of doing things. After studying this a few days with the supervisor, who up to that point had been enthusiastic, the cause became apparent: the supervisor was having difficulty managing the statistical control of the process as he had never used a calculator before. This was a real lesson in personnel management; never assume anything about anyone without checking and the key to success is usually in making sure the individual has the skills and training and the right tools to do the job.

After the machine bottleneck issue had been resolved the process of improvement gained momentum, especially after the first bonus checks were paid at the end of the quarter. The bonus checks were not a huge amount of money but staff had never received bonuses before.

The raw material issue was extremely difficult to resolve. The solution was to store as much as possible inside, test all the material before it entered the manufacturing process, and dispose of all damaged material. Testing all materials and disposing of damaged materials was an expensive process.

Financial & Administration

Survival was the key concern for the shareholders and investors, and short-term survival was dependent on cash flow. In these circumstances new equity or loans are extremely difficult and often impossible to arrange in a timely manner and, if available, too expensive. Therefore, the most immediate need was to manage internal financial resources. This required a careful look at every line item of expenditures and costs of manufacturing. In addition, the Income Statement was adversely affected by write-downs of damaged rubber inventory and obsolete parts, although write-downs were a non-cash expense.

Health & Safety

The company provided constant education of the supervisors about the costs of accidents in human suffering, insurance penalties and production delays after an accident; however, it was finally necessary to fire one of the longest serving supervisors who had been extremely loyal to the previous family management during some tough times.

Sales

In order to diversify the revenue and reduce dependence on GM, Ford and Chrysler, the company initiated contacts with the North American plants of the Asian and European auto manufacturers and new business was under development with them. Substantial effort was also made to find non-automotive uses for recycled tire materials, but large volume applications were difficult to find.

Results

The actions on manufacturing and personnel issues had a very positive, cumulative effect: machine downtime was much reduced, quality was improved, production volumes were increased without a significant investment in new machinery, manpower levels were steady with no major layoffs, and cash flow improved. At the end of the consultant's year-long contract analysis of the financial results confirmed the previous forecasted results and demonstrated support for the assurances of future profitability. Discussions between the company and its lenders concluded with refinancing the existing debt and the provision of new financing that was used to start another tire shredding facility in another location.

Commentary on the case

This is a fascinating case study. It is not about financial re-engineering or a proposal under bankruptcy laws to negate corporate debts. It is not about marketing or strategy, although marketing and strategy were not ignored. This case study is about fixing operations and the resolution of people issues. In fact, implicit in the case study is the idea that the people make the company successful or unsuccessful. The case study is largely silent on management departures but it is reasonable to imagine that there was rotation in the managerial echelon. The comment about the maintenance manager who had been working under difficult circumstances raises the observation that sometimes a worker or a manager's biggest impediment is his or her boss, and changing bosses can in itself raise performance and productivity. Managing in a multi-ethnic environment in a basically peaceful and tolerant society like Canada is a challenge; it is a daunting challenge in societies with greater ethnic or linguistic stresses.

Another fascinating feature of this case study is the expectations of the shareholders. There clearly were two different sets of expectations: the sons had expectations of consumption and the venture capital fund had expectations of medium to long-term increases in share value. These different expectations would normally lead to different behaviors and, in time, to conflict if one or both sets of expectations were unsatisfied. The case study is silent on the relative power of each shareholder but commonly the institutional investor has the shares or the relationship with lenders to force strategic and managerial changes.

Another fascinating observation is that operational improvements were achieved with simple changes. No doubt implementing the simple changes was complicated by the linguistic and ethnic composition of the workforce and by the lack of managerial and supervisory sophistication; nonetheless, the changes were technologically simple. The company did not buy expensive, state-of-the-art equipment and did not incur large capital expenditures. The improvements were achieved by looking at the basics of materials handling and flow, and production equipment scheduling.

Health and safety was obviously important. In this case – and in many other situations – supervisors and workers did not want to change unsafe practices. It could be argued that a turnaround cannot be achieved until the corporate culture is changed, and that one of the deepest embedded components of corporate culture is the collective attitude to health and safety. Patience with violations of basic, common sense health and safety practices should be very short; train, coach and motivate – and terminate those who do not commit to and adhere to safe work practices. However, there is another side to health & safety issues: management must change its own mindset from production at any cost and any risk to a mindset that health and safety must never be sacrificed.

Overall, the transformation within twelve months was a remarkable achievement.

CHAPTER 5: THE BIG BANG: PRICING

Re-pricing of all customer-product combinations is arguably the single most profitable action that the Turnaround CEO can take. It requires a lot of work and raising prices during a turnaround – or a recession – is counter-intuitive but the benefits are huge. In some cases, intelligent re-pricing will resolve the financial component of the turnaround; of course, there will still be human resource issues (after all, who was responsible for systemic bad pricing?) and probably operations, marketing and other issues.

Overcoming a fear of customer price resistance may enable some companies to double pre-tax income. Privately held companies view themselves as price-takers, not price-setters - meaning that they believe that they do not have the market clout to raise prices. (Nokia's pricing is restricted by competition, too.) There is a natural reluctance to raise prices and to risk losing customers; however, pricing to marginal customers and on marginal products should be increased or the costs should be decreased. In some turnarounds intelligent, aggressive re-pricing may add 2% - 5% of sales to pre-tax income. In other cases, the gains to income may be less; however, intelligent re-pricing will correct random over-pricing of some accounts, which makes those accounts vulnerable to competitors, and random under-pricing, which makes those accounts inadequately profitable.

Customer-Product Contribution Margin

The Turnaround CEO does not know if the pricing structure is rational until the pricing structure is, in fact, thoroughly reviewed. Do it promptly and intelligently. If need be, assign or hire on a contract basis the most analytical, numerate person you can find and don't be hesitant about the cost: the pay-off is potentially huge. It is ideal to have a sophisticated analysis of each customer / product contribution margin; however, the practical realities are that sometimes a reasonable calculation may be the best that can be managed in a tight time frame, and on that basis certain prices may be increased sharply. Excessive pricing to certain customers may need to be gradually reduced. This first round of price adjustments must be based on data gathering and specific allocations of reasonably attributable variable costs for every customer-product. Data gathering and analysis may take at least one day of a skilled person's time per $1,000,000 in sales.

Pricing Decisions

Once the customer-product contribution margins are calculated, the Turnaround CEO must chair a team that examines every customer-product account and makes decisions on which accounts to re-price and by how much. Inevitably there will be anxious debate and even shock that key accounts may be re-priced by 5% or 20%. There will assertions that losing an account would be bad for morale (possibly true for a short time) or that the lost volume would harm the company's purchasing power (again, possibly true but often not true) or that the lost volume would send the wrong message to the marketplace (the marketplace usually doesn't care). Implementation must be planned: when to announce the price adjustments, when to make the changes effective, how to communicate the changes to staff and customers, how to train staff to respond to customers. After six months or so, a second, more precise calculation of the profitability of all customers and products will reflect previous re-pricing, the implementation of cost savings and improved information systems.

Price-volume sensitivity

A classic approach to pricing is to measure elasticity of demand - which means the amount that demand changes when prices change. Price sensitivity may be asymmetrical, meaning that if unit volume decreases 2.5% due to a 1.0% price increase, volume may not increase 2.5% if the price is cut 1.0%. Surprisingly, some privately held companies might raise prices on a one-time basis by 1% - 5% more than inflation without imperiling unit sales.

In practice, most turnaround companies will not have sophisticated staff with available time to do price and volume sensitivity research and tests; senior managers should use their managerial expertise and intuition to estimate the impact on profitability.

Price & volume sensitivity

	Base Case	Price Insensitive	Price Sensitive	Price Sensitive
Price Increase:		1.00%	1.00%	-1.00%
Unit Volume Change:		0.00%	-2.50%	2.50%
Unit Price	$60.00	$60.60	$60.60	$59.40
Unit Costs	$37.00	$37.00	$37.00	$37.00
Units	100,000	100,000	97,500	102,500
Revenue	$6,000,000	$6,060,000	$5,908,500	$6,088,500
Total unit costs	$3,700,000	$3,700,000	$3,607,500	$3,792,500
Overhead	$2,000,000	$2,000,000	$2,000,000	$2,000,000
Pre-tax Profit	$300,000	$360,000	$301,000	$296,000

Price re-allocation

Not-for-profit or community organizations face price allocation issues. Here's an example: the new managing editor / publisher of a gay and lesbian community newspaper, part of a larger organization, collected data on the free and discounted advertisements that the newspaper had provided in the previous year. He found that the total cost at standard rates was about equal to the newspaper's annual income. Since the newspaper had a specific vision and mandate, he decided to maintain that level of sponsorship; however, further analysis showed that 10 of the 35 organizations receiving free or discounted advertising were no longer new or impoverished. The decision was made to reduce the discounts to the ten least impoverished organizations and to use the increased revenue to provide free or discounted advertising to more needy organizations.

Price cuts

Price cuts make sense to liquidate end-of-season fashion merchandise, overstocks of any product and products in danger of becoming obsolete, and to correct any accounts that are over-priced. Price cuts to gain market share are a high-risk strategy and should be used with caution; they can erode or destroy profitability and may trigger an industry price war.

Incremental pricing

Incremental pricing means pricing one order to cover its costs plus some overhead. It may have merit for a unique order that would not expose a business to a perceived betrayal of existing customers or to the corporate disease of frequent discounting.

Price Wars

Price wars are an opportunity to ruin a viable industry. Price wars are bleeding contests. Turnaround companies rarely have the financial resources to withstand a price war and should rarely or never start a price war.

Three basic responses to a competitor's price cuts

- Maintaining prices may have no impact on unit sales if the competitor's price cut is minor, if product differentiation is great or if the cost to the customer of switching suppliers is greater than the perceived benefit. If those conditions do not apply, unit volumes may fall and profits may decrease but the decrease may be minor compared to lost profits if a price cut is made. Do a price – volume sensitivity analysis, even if imperfect, before matching competitors' price decreases.

- Matching the competitor's price cut may maintain unit volumes, result in lower profits and even losses and signal the competitor that any further price reductions will be matched and that a price war will not gain the competitor market share.

- Exceeding the competitor's price cut may provoke a further spiral of price cuts, leading to industry-wide losses and little re-allocation of unit volumes and market share.

If the Turnaround CEO is leading a turnaround during a recession, all the options are unattractive but resisting price cuts may be the wiser decision – and it will take guts because staff will invariably argue hard for matching price cuts.

CHAPTER 6: THE CORE LUBRICANT: MARKETING[10]

Turnarounds must focus on finances, and Turnaround CEOs often have finance or legal backgrounds. The focus on the accountants' paradigm is inevitable in the early stages of a turnaround; however, even in the earliest stages of a turnaround, marketing and operations should be inputs to decision-making. As the turnaround progresses, marketing and operations must become increasingly central considerations.

After – and only after – ridding the company of unproductive marketing and sales expenditures and after – and only after – intelligently re-pricing all customer-product accounts, it is time to start upgrading basic marketing efforts. Upgrading marketing tactics will likely start after six months of a disciplined turnaround. For companies with seriously flawed operations, the Turnaround CEO may be forced to delay marketing upgrades until operational problems are solved. In those cases where the core problem that caused the descent into the turnaround position is, in fact, marketing, then analyzing and addressing the marketing function should be early on the agenda.

Early Phase Actions

Marketing is the focus on satisfying customers - profitably. Focus means positive, conscious, purposeful, directed and coherent action. Satisfying customers means a positive sense of good value received and an absence of irritants in the pre-sale, purchase and post-sale experience. Profitably means that the companies know the costs of making products and serving customers and charge enough to generate a reasonable return on equity. High profit customers, high potential customers and unprofitable customers should be priced and served appropriately. Marketing companies are smart companies that focus and manage their scarce resources.

---

[10] © Rick Morgan

Customer profiles & segments

Customer and customer category profiles may inspire fresh, creative marketing programs. List all characteristics of each customer or customer category. For consumers, list the usual demographic information (age, gender, marital status, language, religion, income, health, education, political and social affiliations and brand loyalty). For industrial customers, list corporate information (sales, profitability, purchases of similar products, competitive position, purchasing patterns, brand loyalty and payment patterns). For each customer or customer category, list how to satisfy needs (the selling process, delivery, packaging, product features, pricing, payment terms). Then, list all possible actions that the company might take to satisfy each customer or customer category. Recognize, plan and act appropriately for each unique market segment.

Archetypes of customers and potential customers.

- Who's Buying Dinner? - The good customers.
- Who'll Buy Lots Of Dinners? The high potential customers.
- Who's Eating Dinner? - The over-served and under-priced customers.
- Who's Stealing Dinner? - The bad debts and slow payers.
- We'll Buy Dinner This Time - The one-time discount customers.
- The Giant In The Sleeping Bag - The dominant customer.
- The Marginal Customers, because of us and them.
- The Marginal Customers, because of us.
- The Used To Bees - Customers who no longer buy from us.
- The Should Bees - Customers who aren't but should be.
- The Soon To Bees - The emerging customers.

Market research

Old marketing programs cause the decline of companies. Retail customers grow old, die and move. Industrial customers expand, downsize, re-organize and re-locate. Therefore, yesterday's marketing programs may target yesterday's customers. Research and analysis can pinpoint exciting new opportunities, and sometimes spending the money on professional research is desirable. Of course, the cheapest and best market research is often the careful analysis and survey of a company's current customers. If the Turnaround CEO has identified marketing as a major cause of the corporate malaise or as a major lever to revitalize the company, then he or she should be meeting customers as much as possible, as soon as possible. The information gained through these contacts will constitute invaluable, actionable marketing intelligence.

Get rid of the unwise

During the first six months the Turnaround CEO must be watching for any unwise marketing or marketing related activities and any silly inconsistencies that may have quietly crept into the company's informal practices.

In one turnaround, the marketing department had printed baseball caps with company logos, but those caps were only given to important customers as prizes for golf days and Christmas parties. The delivery drivers – who met customers every day - were equipped with company shirts, pants and jackets but they wore baseball caps of other trucking companies and sports teams. So the decision was made to give every driver two dozen baseball caps with company logos - and told that if they were going to wear caps, it would be company caps. They were also encouraged to give out caps to warehouse or factory staff of customers who gave them access or signed their delivery slips so that the company's name and logo would permeate customers' workplaces. Of note, there was no system of reporting or auditing of baseball cap use (turnaround companies do not need more bureaucracy). This was an obvious and inexpensive way to drive consistency of the company's image and spread it across its customer base.

In another instance, the turnaround company prided itself – with limited justification – that it was the best in the industry. A driver commented one day that the chemical delivery trucks were starting to look poorly maintained. The trucks were in fact well-maintained in terms of mechanical performance and safety, but the areas of the trucks most exposed to chemical mist or leakage were pitted with flaking paint and scabs of rust. The company promptly started a program of sandblasting and painting the surfaces of every chemical tanker – two every month, in order to spread the costs. This program enhanced the company's brand image as well as the self-image of the drivers, a vital constituency of the firm.

In a third case, the company's website was simply awful and amateurish – stale-dated and in some cases untrue. The website was purged of untruths and updated information was added. This was done inexpensively rather than incurring the cost of a total redesign of the website since the website was not central to the company's marketing.

Get rid of the unproductive

When the sky is falling, as in the austere conditions of a turnaround, any remedial efforts that are not core to survival are a luxury. Sometimes it's uncertain if any marketing is productive or what marketing expenditures are most productive. The focus should be on the identification of what marketing expenditures are most productive.

Start by asking the question 'how much business did this activity or expenditure bring in over the last twelve months?' Unsurprisingly, turnaround companies usually don't know, but asking a group of marketing and sales people should provide a consensus view. In one company, asking that basic question repeatedly resulted in the cancellation of all telephone directory advertising and all magazine advertising – not as a cost savings measure, although the cost savings were appreciated, but because those expenditures did not generate revenue and therefore were a waste of precious resources.

The same company applied the same rigor to the 'dues, memberships and donations' expense, which included the cost of organizations that were primarily environmental, health & safety, marketing and administrative-related. Managers from each department participated in a roundtable discussion. As a result, the environmental and health & safety dues, memberships and donations were slightly changed, but the marketing and administrative-related components were cut by 70% and 45% respectively.

Another question that is tough and useful is: 'if we were not doing this, would we start to do it at this point?' If the answer is negative, then the activity and associated cost should be cancelled (not just reduced unless the cost of canceling and later resumption would be prohibitive).

And, another question is 'who is unproductive?' The answer may be clear: do a ranking of each marketing and sales person: divide an individual's total sales or, better, contribution margin (sales minus attributable variable costs) by the person's salary plus benefits; then, rank the individuals from most productive to least productive. Obviously, anyone whose ratio is 1:1 or less is sitting on an ejection seat.

However, investing the time to take the analysis of an individual's contribution to a higher level of sophistication is desirable and more equitable to the individual. Who has the better territories or product lines? Who has more house accounts as opposed to fiercely competitive accounts? In other words, why are there differences in the productivity of marketing and sales personnel? It may be that one or more individuals have challenging territories or product lines. Apparently productive staff may have comparatively easy workloads and some may simply be unsuited to the current or anticipated future environment. These additional factors are important in decisions about who to terminate and who to retain.

Gaining Traction

As turnarounds gain traction with tangible improvement to the balance sheet and income statement, marketing & sales become key drivers of the Consolidation of Progress. Managers can save to survival - they cannot save to prosperity. Once a company has progressed to the Consolidation of Progress phase, money must be spent on marketing & sales. To be simplistic – marketing is merely about giving customers more of what they want - at the time, place and price they want to pay. Marketing enables and enhances an enterprise to sell its goods and services. It is the core lubricant.

Marketing communications, in all its forms, messages and media can play a vital role in countering the "loser" image of a company in turnaround. Nobody wants to lend to a loser, buy from a loser, work for a loser – have anything to do with a loser. Also, people like to pass along bad news or negative impressions. It's all basic human nature.

Managing marketing communications efforts effectively is very important in shaping perceptions of all those significant others who impact the welfare of the company. It's necessary to not only do the right things and have the right results, but to appear to be doing so. This role is extremely important to a successful turnaround and needs to be done effectively if pragmatically. There are many ingredients and tools available in the marketing mix, including messages to stakeholders both inside and outside the company. These opportunities are discussed in more detail in Chapter 7.

Within the turnaround agenda, questions need to be answered in order to have a better handle on the current reality – and diagnose the current health of customer relationships. Even as the analysis, restructuring and re-engineering of the company is underway, the company is exposed and vulnerable to defection of customers and staff. Retention is fundamentally important, followed by customer profitability and growth in share of wallet / requirements and, finally, growth through acquisition of new customers. The basic questions to answer (or confirm) in order to plan marketing strategies and tactics are all customer-focused.

Basic questions to plan marketing strategies and tactics

- Who is the customer? What are their wants, needs, culture, history?
- What are their key product / service requirements?
- How tough is our competition? What's their / our competitive edge?
- Who are our profitable customers? How healthy are our relationships?
- What value does our company provide? Is it unique compared to the competition?
- How do we monitor results and adjust our efforts?

The marketing audit

Review all activities in place within the marketing mix – review the product and service offering and terminate the weak movers and budget drainers (including the drain of management attention and anxiety). If these components have contractual issues, continue and / or negotiate an exit agreement with the customers.

Review, rationalize and / or adjust your pricing strategy. Review your channel relationships and revitalize as required. Review and freeze any discretionary promotion spending that doesn't support short-term transactions. Focus on promotion spending instead of advertising where possible, to support sales and leads. Under turnaround conditions, when you're bailing the boat, it's no time for new brand building efforts.

Review your staffing expense and outsourcing contracts. You may be over-staffed. The outside suppliers may be too costly or simply no longer needed. In fact, the quality of what has been going on may be deficient. As previously noted, often the conditions leading up to the need for turning around a company are chronic and widespread practices of inefficiency or ineffectiveness. In summary, your staff and vendors may no longer be appropriate given the need for retrenchment and maintenance style marketing.

Doing more with less

The strategy for turnarounds is to be tactical – keeping prerequisite tools in place with as little expense as possible. Synergies are particularly important in turnarounds and are achieved where marketing components are consistent and integrated. This means that the same messages are repeated wherever they are conveyed. At a minimum this provides power of reinforcement. The repertoire of communications tools is wide and varied. The messages must consistently convey and support the business and its strategy. No matter how incidental the communications tool, consistency and synergy are keys to successful marketing under austerity – and, this consistently extends to such items as business cards, hats, mugs and truck signage. Use the various tools with prudence, focus and selectively.

Use Marketing Tools Smartly

- *Name, Logo, Symbol:* review and make consistent any and all branding materials so that all identification appears the same, i.e., comes from the same company. The cost of new supplies can be reduced by dropping colors or printing fewer copies or targeting only key customers.
- *Competition:* analyze and monitor the competition –advance beyond whatever marketing or communications tactics competitors are using.
- *Product:* review your product / service line-up and rationalize – but don't add or fill any gaps unless absolutely necessary. Every penny must be used wisely.
- *Package/Display*: evaluate your packaging and use up whatever materials are in stock – plan and redesign in order to strengthen your retail presence when reprinting is scheduled.
- *Advertising:* freeze all spending unless you have unbreakable channel promises or contractual arrangements with the media – or where retail promotional support is required (brand building programs can come later when funds are available).
- *Promotion:* continue selectively, if the payout has an established track record, with incremental sales or leads for the program– a turnaround is clearly not the time for experimentation.
- *Word-of-mouth:* initiate communications, through personal and business connections personally (email and phone and snail mail) – this is a powerful, inexpensive tool for outbound messaging which should be conducted by as many of the staff as appropriate, with the goal of encouraging positive news about the re-emerging or rebounding company.
- *Publicity/media relations:* in the later phase of a successful turnaround there will be good news to be communicated. If there has been an adverse event of media interest, publicity / media relations will be important. See Chapter 7.
- *Website:* review and redesign your website to be current, relevant, useable, since your site is such an important "face to your market". Fortunately, this tool can be upgraded cost-effectively, since there are many good designers available. Websites often languish when they aren't core to the business and marketing activities, and often are not reviewed and revised during turnarounds.

- *Brochures:* consider a "turnaround" story brochure as part of the communications strategy. See Chapter 7.
- *Collateral Materials*: review all your other materials and activities and curtail or postpone production if they are not providing essential or value-added support to keep or attract customers.
- *Trade Shows/Conferences:* review and rationalize, only participating, attending and hosting where the events are core to current relationships or business development.

Living The Brand

You, as well as your employees, need to show on a daily basis that you're open for business (contrary to rumors). You need to appear confident and strong, and that you are in the game for the long haul. The personal "moment of truth" when managers or even the rank and file are in touch with "outsiders" is crucial. Customers can sense disgruntlement and anxiety among your employees. Any negative impressions or experiences as they filter through the market by word of mouth will lose you business, damage your reputation and weaken the momentum of the turnaround.

Understand that during a turnaround, staff morale suffers ongoing negative pressure. Alignment is tough enough without clear, consistent updates on what's going on with the surgery and whatever other remedial actions are underway. You need to nurture the staff who remain after the restructuring, who suffer from "survivors' syndrome". You need to reduce their continuing anxiety by regular contact and updates on the progress of the turnaround. There's no magic schedule, since turnaround circumstances are more or less volatile and company sizes vary. However, every couple of weeks during the "height of the action" would probably be most beneficial. Also, town hall gatherings allow the Turnaround CEO to deliver the updates personally. Always include opportunities for questions from staff.

Channels Of Distribution

The channels of distribution are usually very important to manufacturers – and effectively managing those relationships are one of the keys to success. How a product flows downstream to the ultimate end-user or consumer will influence the industry's and company's cost structure, pricing and volumes. The Turnaround CEO will need to assess which channels and customers within those channels are most critical, and will plan and devote resources appropriately to the distribution strategy.

Public Relations & Community Service

Public relations is about impressing people outside the company. Public relations can be community service. It can also be media relations and raising the company profile through unpaid activities. It is unrealistic to expect positive public relations when the Turnaround CEO has terminated staff, is cutting expenses and raising prices. Executives of Turnaround companies should consider temporarily dropping all public relations and community service activities or at least minimizing involvement and expenditures on public relations and community service - there is not enough money or time during a turnaround. During a turnaround, a lower community profile is desirable until the company has some good news to share.

The exception (to the general desirability of a lower community profile) is for turnaround situations that are dependent on public support or government largesse or licensing; in those cases, caution and sensitivity are prudent.

CHAPTER 7: THE THREAD THAT BINDS: COMMUNICATION [11]

As the business challenges mount and become more and more unpredictable and urgent, it is vital that management leverages one of its most important and least expensive tools to the fullest extent possible. By managing the messaging in a thoughtful and unemotional way, management has the ability to ensure that the brand remains robust and poised for future growth. Even more importantly, good stewardship of the messages will assist the organization and its individual owners and employees feel good about themselves. It will help ensure that they are able to move forward during and after the crisis at hand.

Start With The End In Mind

As difficult as it may seem in a time of crisis, it is vital that you define what you want people to say about you and your company once the financial crisis has passed. Which statement would you rather have on the street if you were President of Lakeshore Group?

Lakeshore Group has been in default of payments and has taken a real beating in the past 6 months.

OR

Lakeshore Group is consolidating its operations to ensure that it is poised for a strong comeback after its current financial crisis.

The first statement leaves the future of both Lakeshore Group and the supplier or customer in real limbo – uncertainty is always frightening. The second sentence conveys that the management of Lakeshore Group is in complete control of the situation, making strategic decisions that will ensure its competitiveness and ability to move forward. Suppliers and customers will be reassured by this statement knowing that Lakeshore Group will continue to support their businesses going forward. Management has the

---

[11] Ann MacDiarmid ©Raptor Communications Inc.

ability and responsibility to manage the over-arching messages with all of its stakeholder groups. Make sure that your messages are clear, memorable and compelling for each of your stakeholder groups. Always be prompt with your communication. Don't wait for all of the facts because you will never have all of the facts.

Who are you talking to?

Ideally, you will have defined your stakeholder groups many times throughout your business history and will have their demographics and contact numbers in an easily accessible database. If you do not, make a list of every type of stakeholder that your business has and then group your database contact information under these headings.

Minimum list of stakeholder groups

- Employees
- Customers
- Suppliers
- Owners/shareholders
- Board of Directors
- Neighbors
- Family
- Your insurer
- Bankers/Lenders/ Holders of debt
- Professional or industry groups of which you may/may not be a member
- Regulatory bodies governing your industry
- Media – trade media and general interest media as channels to others
- Ex-employees
- Competitors

Robust and well maintained databases of each of these stakeholder groups will be valued assets for your organization on a going basis and are absolutely vital to your ability to communicate through a turnaround or crisis situation.

Allies and enemies

Amongst these stakeholder groups there will likely be some obvious enemies and allies. Your objective is to move all of the enemies from threatening positions to ones of support and trust. At various times in the turnaround, one stakeholder group may be perceived as a threat or enemy – perhaps suppliers or lenders that force payments or repayments. With careful and frequent communication, it is possible and necessary to move them into the ally camp by reassuring them, sharing facts with them, listening to their needs and making sure that they understand how much you are committed to helping them meet their own business goals. It is essential to look forward with all of your communications. Placing blame or finger pointing is never productive. Reinforce supportive behaviors in others and avoid judgmental messages. What do you want people in each of your stakeholder groups to say and do at each of the following stages of the crisis? Make sure you articulate these, write them down and monitor your progress against your desired outcomes.

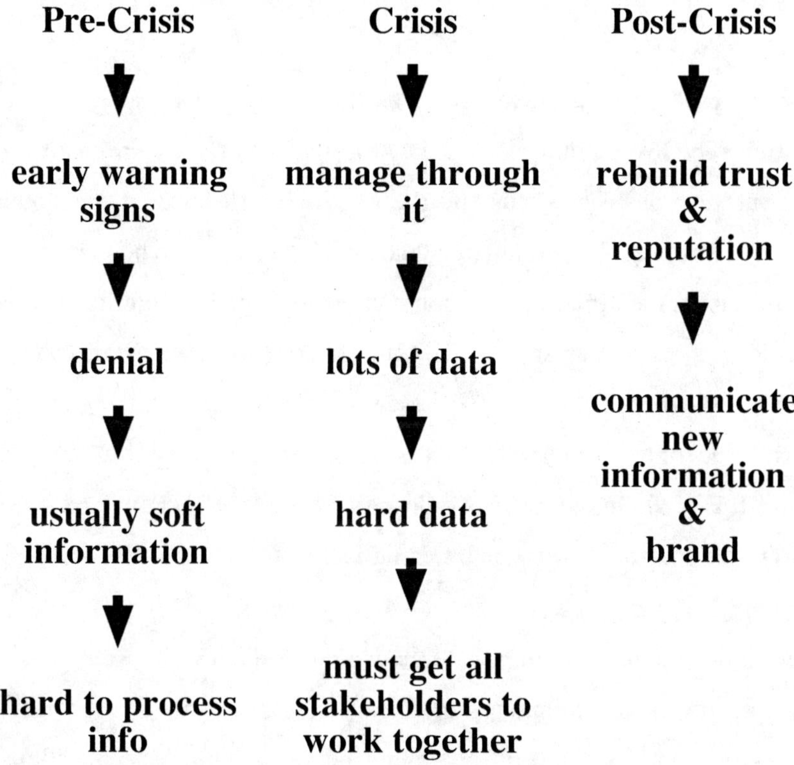

Communication Audit

List all of the various ways that you communicate with each of these stakeholder groups. You will be surprised at how many existing opportunities you have to ensure that they hear the same, consistent message directly from you and your company.

Ways that you and staff likely communicate with suppliers

- Telephone answering – in person receptionist or automated voice mail.
- The signage outside of your office is likely seen regularly by their delivery personnel.
- Interface with your staff at receiving.
- The payment checks you send to them; the envelopes they are mailed in and there is always an opportunity to insert a letter into the envelope.
- Your website.
- Your company newsletter.
- An industry newsletter.
- Industry conventions and meetings.

Make a list for each of your stakeholders so that you can take advantage of existing communication vehicles to reinforce your key messages and to ensure that they feel fully informed about your business status and the impact it will have on their own business goals. Create a communications matrix that matches each stakeholder group with the communication tools identified in your communications audit. Refer to it whenever you are communicating with your stakeholders and choose the best media from those that already exist. Different types of messages require different types of delivery mechanisms. The more complex the message, the more likely you will need to use written tools. It is vital that your stakeholders know the facts and not be allowed to jump to conclusions that may or may not be based on fact.

In addition to leveraging existing communication vehicles, it is important that all communication – even with suppliers and customers – be two-way. Make sure that each stakeholder group has a way to communicate with you, ask questions or seek clarification. It may be a dedicated voice mail or email or an old-fashioned suggestion box at the front door. Whatever you set up, make sure that it is checked daily and that all of the inquiries are responded to within 48 hours. Make certain that the key messages are being repeated regularly and consistently. Those that ask questions must feel free to ask them anonymously and be reassured that there will never be any risk to them for expressing concerns. Fear of reprisal from management will disconnect employees and other stakeholders when you most need them to be engaged in the business and trusting of management.

Share the key messages verbally and in writing with all of your staff – every single one of them has the ability and opportunity to tell your story to someone – either in the course of their regular work or after hours in casual conversation. Make sure that everyone has a copy of the key messages, knows that only those messages can be repeated and that if they disagree in any way, they should discuss the issues internally with you or their immediate superior.

<u>Depend on the facts – make sure that they are credible</u>

During a turnaround situation, it is virtually guaranteed that you and your senior management team will be very busy, having to juggle many balls at the same time. It is easy to forget the facts. If the facts are not clear and consistent, the messages will not be credible.

The best insurance against misrepresentation is a Corporate Fact Book which should be prepared by the senior management team, updated regularly and used as a resource by all managers at all meetings – both internal and external. This fact book should be well indexed so it is an easy reference for all queries.

A well-prepared fact book is an essential tool at all meetings. When you refer to it, the audiences will be reassured that you are well prepared to answer questions. It will also ensure that everyone on the management team has exactly the same facts and figures at their fingertips. Using it as a trusted resource should be mandatory. Talking about numerical and financial details off the top of your head when you are stressed is inexcusable and very risky. Manage the details through your fact book. Keep the details small. Record them all. Keep them up to date and relevant to the issues at hand.

Minimum contents of Corporate Fact Book

- Recent financial statements.
- Up to date cash flow – actual to date and pro forma for 2 years.
- Sales statistics – past and projected.
- Organization charts and staffing numbers by department.
- The most recent business plan.
- The key messages discussed above.
- The guiding principles, value statements for the company.
- Inventory numbers.
- Product or service descriptions.
- A comprehensive set of questions and answers (Q&A) for each stakeholder group.
- The latest annual report – if one exists.
- Competitive analysis or analysis of your market positioning. This might be in the form of a SWOT (Strengths, Weaknesses, Opportunities and Threats) analysis.
- Telephone numbers and emergency contact numbers for the management team, key advisors (lawyers, accountants, lenders).

Protect Your Brand

Your brand is far more than the name of your organization or its graphic representation / logo. It is the emotional connection that people have to your products, services and company. It is a distillation of who you are; what you believe in; how you behave and what you communicate.

Your brand is not a façade. It is the soul of your organization and it will help build a personal relationship between you and your stakeholders. During a time of crisis, your brand should continue to guide all of your behaviors and messages.

brand = your image = your core promise

Because you should have already articulated your brand values and core promises, it should be easy to refer back to these every time you ask for support or craft a key message. Is what you are asking for or telling people consistent with your existing brand promise? If not, why not?

"How you act toward individuals and firms around you will not be forgotten and will often be rewarded in the long run. Bad treatment or inconsistent treatment of your customers, suppliers, distributors or regulators in a way that does not espouse your brand values only works to depreciate your brand."[12]

Your principles – both as an individual and as the leader of an organization – will help you keep an even keel during a time of financial and business stress. You should feel so comfortable with your brand promise that it becomes your very best friend as you weather the turnaround and crisis.

Your brand is also the heart of future growth and stability. It is your reputation and can be an important tangible asset for potential lenders and financial supporters. People do not react positively to a blemished brand. Care for your brand. Protect it and nurture it at all times. Nurture relationships so that they are solid and based on trust as you move beyond the business crisis.

Your brand is communicated every day in how people and organizations interact with your company whether it is in person or driving by your plant or offices. The feeling that is conveyed by the signage, the spoken word and the tonality is key to moving stakeholders from being enemies to becoming allies.

---

[12] Muzyka, Daniel F., Sauder School of Business, University of British Columbia and Weiss, Lawrence A., McDonough School of Business, Georgetown University, To succeed in the hurricane: Globe and Mail, October 27, 2008, page B6.

Emotional Times

As difficult as it may be in times of crisis, the tonality that should govern all communications internally and externally through a financial crisis must be:

Calm **Honest Heartfelt** **Consistent**

When your business is in a turnaround situation, you are very likely to be emotionally fragile, physically exhausted and uncertain of your own future. It is at these times, that it is most difficult to remain calm, cool and collected – but you must if you are going to be demonstrating the needed leadership qualities to get your staff, customers, suppliers and family to be your faithful allies.

It is important that you take stock of your own emotional state regularly and do whatever you need to in order to ensure that the decisions you are making are based on the cold hard facts and not emotionally charged. "Executives who encounter corporate distress often go through the same emotional stages as dying people: denial, anger, bargaining, depression and finally acceptance."[13]

Know where you and your key colleagues are on this emotional roller coaster and deal with your state of mind. For some business owners, this means seeking the counsel of a therapist or personal coach. For others, it means devoting extra time to physical fitness and programmed relaxation (massages, meditation). Whatever it takes, make time for it as a priority in your business success.

Sometimes a trusted friend or former partner can play a mentoring role to the CEO who finds herself in a financial or business crisis. If you choose to leverage such a relationship to help you through the business crisis, make sure that you define the

---

[13] Turnaround Management Association, www.turnaround.org/Assistance/Industry_Renewal.aspx

parameters of the coaching or mentoring role at the very outset to ensure that it will not affect your long-term friendship with that person.

In stressful meetings with key stakeholders (like creditors, bankers or staff) it is far easier to be unemotional if you are well prepared for the meeting. Set and share written agendas, script yourself with written talk notes, refer regularly to your fact book and define exactly what outcome you want from that meeting. Stick to the message and don't let your adversaries change the direction of the meeting. If they do, refer them back to the agenda – which they should have agreed to at the outset of the meeting. This grounding allows you to be as unemotional as possible.

Equally important as controlling your own emotional state and appearance is reading the emotions of your stakeholders. Are your creditors at risk of losing their business if you default on your payments? If so, they may be showing some fear and anger. Be empathetic to their needs but stay on your message. Try to move them from the adversary enemy camp into the ally camp by offering to work out innovative solutions together. Do your very best to show them that you are on their side. Encourage them to remove their emotions from their communications and their own decision-making. This is especially important with staff that may be at risk of losing their jobs, with investors that may be losing their financial security and with family members. These are important allies who need to see you as a calm and honest partner who is dedicated to helping them with demonstrable examples of your brand values and principles.

You must be able to confidently lead your stakeholders though the rough waters. If your facts and messages are consistent and credible, you will have built solid foundations of trust and honesty that will allow you to move forward in your business and as an individual. It is important to hold your head high as the process unfolds. Many people and organizations are looking to you for leadership and expect you to model the behavior you expect from them. Once the storm has passed, be proud of the decisions you made, value the allies that you can now count on because of how you treated them throughout the process and move on confidently. Now is the time to seek their support in defining a new strategic plan for you and your business.

Spending money on communications during a financial crisis

Generally, investing in new communication tools and channels need not be a priority when cash is extremely tight. In times of crisis, focus on existing communication tools that you have identified in your communication audit. Don't get into creating new tools that could take you away from the key financial priorities. Leverage these existing communication channels creatively to share your messages with each of your stakeholder groups.

Expensive outsourced public relations plans can generally wait until your business is on solid financial footing and new communication objectives are outlined in a forward looking strategic plan. However, this does assume that the basic of stakeholder databases and a communication audit are in place within your organization and that you and your management team can jointly identify key messages, prepare the fact books and reply to staff, supplier and customer questions. If not, then it is strongly recommended that you consider hiring a crisis communications professional. If you do so, it is important to define the scope of the consulting assignment to ensure that you both understand the relationship, expectations and outcomes. Neither you nor the consultant wants a professional relationship to suffer from "assignment creep". You do not need a crisis communications professional coaching you on financial tools or inventory management. Neither do they want to be asked to take over staff newsletters or accounts receivable unless you have scoped that as a requirement.

Most professionals will scope their assignment to meet your needs and provide an hourly or daily rate. Check their references with other companies that have used them in similarly challenging times, make sure that you have a confidentiality agreement in place and be prepared to share 100% of your business facts with them. Only with a complete understanding of your business challenges can they be expected to advise you and help you reach the desired outcomes. Pay for advisors that are trained to ask the most difficult questions and help you work through the answers. A good crisis communications professional will be comfortable delivering frank honest messages to all of the stakeholders.

Avoid being talked into buying new communication tools until the fundamentals of your business are solid.

It is often important to manage the media carefully. Never view the media or what it says as a crisis. The media is interested because there is a crisis. If you identify and fix the real problem, the media will go away. If the media story isn't what you want, then you have not communicated the facts properly. Remember, the media is not an audience – just a channel to other stakeholders. Never use the media as a channel to employees, unions, customers or suppliers. Face to face communication with these groups is essential and the CEO or Chair is usually the best spokesperson with these key stakeholders. Secrecy with any of these groups makes the story bigger. Transparency demonstrates honesty and trust.

Readiness Preparedness

Throughout this chapter, we have referred to several basic communication tools that you should have in place – whether or not you are facing a turnaround situation. They will serve you and your business in very good stead if you ensure that you have the following in place and up to date as part of your regular business operations.

Effective crisis management is the "planned ability to act quickly and decisively to regain technical control and respond/inform in a way that is honest, timely, credible, caring and socially responsible."[14]

---

[14] The Mindszenthy & Roberts Corporation, Toronto, Boards in Crisis Conference, Institute of Corporate Directors, November 2005.

Basic communication tools

- Stakeholder database – a list of all of your stakeholders, their key contact information, sortable by stakeholder type.
- Communication audit – a list of all of the existing communication tools that touch each of your stakeholder groups. Keep a copy of the most up to date version of each tool for easy referral.
- Communication matrix - that matches stakeholder groups with the existing communication tools and messages.
- Corporate fact book – a well organized hard copy of the key aspects of your business that you and your management team can rely on to be up-to-date, correct and consistent.
- Two-way stakeholder engagement process - to engage stakeholders in the business issues.
- Statements of brand values, vision, mission and core promises.
- Crisis communication protocol – although a robust crisis communication plan is always desirable, many small businesses cannot anticipate the crises that could befall them. However, you can decide in advance:
    - Who will be the decision maker in the event of a crisis?
    - Who will be the internal and external spokesperson for the organization?
    - Who needs to know about the crisis? When?
    - How will the key stakeholders be informed that there is a crisis?
    - Are there some urgent actions that need to be taken to protect the organization? What are they?

In summary, communicate, communicate and communicate in an open, transparent and honest way. Be accurate. Be on the spot. Be proactive. Leverage your ethics and integrity to build credibility regardless of the outcome of the turnaround of your business.

Having managed through a turnaround or financial crisis both you and your organization will have been through enormous change. If all is managed carefully, the organization's sense of community will still be intact if "the changes have been executed in a way that the people affected not only see it as right for the business, but believe that it has been managed in a way that honors their contribution, treats them fairly and gives them the opportunity for the best possible future career."[15] This is what really matters.

---

[15] What Really Matters; Service Leadership, People and Values, John Peppers, First Yale University Press, 2007, page 150.

CHAPTER 8: OVERHAULING THE ENGINE: OPERATIONS

Many successful turnarounds involve substantial improvements to or adjustments in operations. There is an old comment that General Motors started its long deterioration when 'car men' stopped running the company and finance men started running it. Companies must be good at what they do.

Turnaround companies rarely are good at operations. That's at least part of the reason why customers do not buy enough of their products or are unwilling to pay enough to allow the companies to achieve profitability. Splashy marketing or sophisticated customer segmentation may be helpful; but, in the end, the customer must be satisfied with the product or service.

Operations require stability and predictability. Manufacturers do not frequently change processes, machine configurations or schedules. Trucking companies follow historical precedent when setting routes. Retailers repeat past merchandising of seasonal items. Restaurants greet, seat and serve customers the same way, day after day. The bureaucracy of quality programs makes processes rigid; the documentation and administration of ISO is onerous for many companies and becomes a straightjacket that restricts improvements; the goal becomes adherence to ISO rather than using ISO to help improve. (For the record, ISO and similar programs are excellent; it is the users of those programs who do not use them correctly and creatively.) The result is that operations staff may be the most resistant to change and, hence, the most in need of coaching, goading and pressuring by the Turnaround CEO.

Get The Data, Set The Benchmarks

As soon as possible – within four to six weeks of starting a turnaround – the process of evaluating operations must start. The Turnaround CEO should delegate to one person or a small group the task of comparing the company's operations with others in the industry.

Published reports and credit reports are useful. Most jurisdictions have reports on waste disposal. It is possible to compare companies' waste disposal by chemical and bi-product and deduce efficiencies and environmental recoveries. Here is one example of getting and using publicly available information: the Turnaround CEO of a distributor asked the controller to download summaries of provincial vehicle safety reports and vehicle inspection reports of the company's competitors. The summaries revealed that the company was not the best in its industry, with implications for health & safety and insurance costs. The controller then downloaded those summaries monthly, prepared statistical comparisons of the company and its competitors and distributed the monthly statistical comparisons to senior management and the board of directors.

Here is another example of getting external data. A small, single location grocery retailer was under pressure from its bank. The turnaround consultant was not a grocery expert, but he did have a fresh pair of eyes. He insisted that the storeowner accompany him for a day while he toured the three largest and best grocery retailers in the area. By noon, after only two competitors had been visited, the owner and the consultant identified a number of things that could be done fast and cheaply to improve merchandising.

In other cases, benchmarks can be based on internal data. A manufacturer can sift through historical data and compile the material conversion, re-work and inventory turnover ratios for the preceding year or five years; setting goals for improvement and measuring improvement is then fairly easy. A distributor can track order fill rates, contribution margin per delivery mile or kilometer, truck load and go time, and so on. One distributor found that off-loading incoming material and loading out-bound trucks was expensive; analysis showed that incoming deliveries were scheduled early in the morning because staff handling incoming loads liked to go home early, which meant that they had a relaxed early afternoon and were unavailable, or available at overtime rates, to load delivery trucks when the delivery trucks returned in the mid-afternoon. A simple change in scheduling of incoming loads and staff saved significant overtime costs.

Report the benchmarks & monthly results

Operational benchmarks and monthly results should be reported as widely as possible. The reports might be simple, clear graphs that show material conversion rates, accident rates or defect and re-work rates. What is important must be measured and reported every day or week to managers and every week or month to the CEO. Managers should provide written explanations of remedial actions. The Turnaround CEO must follow up on the reports on a regular basis – at least monthly or, if operations is a major weakness, every week. If operations is key to a successful turnaround, highlights should be reported monthly to the board of directors.

Get Grease Under Your Fingernails

The Turnaround CEO must spend time in the company's manufacturing plants, its distribution centers and its retail stores. He or she must ride on the trucks of long distance haulers or be in the logging camps of forestry companies. There is no substitute for devoting as much time as possible to on-site visits. How much time? Depending on the company, perhaps one to four days / week in the first three months, and then more time or less time depending on the challenges of the paradigms. For greater clarity, being on-site does not mean spending all the time in a plant's meeting rooms; being on-site means time on the production floor or warehouse with workers, in trucks with drivers, in small meetings with engineers, and in informal meetings with union officials. Being on-site is asking questions and listening to answers. As Rob Evans, a seasoned construction and retail executive, said 'Don't hunker in the bunker.' After three – six months the Turnaround CEO should be able to give a competent, non-technical explanation of all of the company's major processes and be able to distinguish between reasons and excuses for operational problems.

Purchasing, Material Handling & Logistics

Purchasing, like other aspects of turnaround companies, may be antiquated. The decision to make purchasing the first or last component of revitalization of operations depends on how important it is. If purchased inputs account for a high proportion of total costs compared to material handling or processing, then it's a high priority. If there is suspicion that there may be ineffective purchasing or fraud, then it's a high priority. Otherwise, purchasing may be relegated to the twelve-month or later point of the turnaround.

The total cost of moving and storing things may be the last frontier of big savings in well-run companies, and the first big opportunity for turnaround companies. Again, getting the data is vital. Tracking and mapping is advisable. There are many good courses and texts available for staff; the Turnaround CEO will not have time to become as deeply involved as ideal, but he or she must at least ensure that competent staff become involved. Again, setting the benchmarks and measuring progress is vital. The exception is material handling and logistics companies; in those cases, the Turnaround CEO must be involved.

Research & Development, Special Projects

Research & Development and special projects may appear to be dilemmas: should they be shut down in order to conserve cash and help the company survive the next six to twelve months, or should they continue and help the company prepare for recovery and growth? Save the cash now or invest now? Cut or continue? The choice may be bogus. The question is framed as an either / or choice when often the choice is presented too simply and too early.

Questions about R & D and special projects

- What projects are underway?
- Are the projects exploratory or aimed at specific commercialization opportunities? What are those opportunities and possible financial rewards?
- When were the projects started and how much has been invested to date?
- What was the original forecast completion date and total cost?
- What is the current forecast completion date and cost?
- Can any of the projects be fast-tracked or re-oriented to near-term commercialization?

The answers to those questions will indicate if R & D and special projects should be shut down in whole or in part, or if they should continue or even be expanded. (By the way, the amount of past investment in a project is a sunk cost and is not financially relevant; but the amount spent to date compared to the original forecast will show if the engineers and managers are dreamers.)

Another choice is stopping the pursuit of perfection, and just telling the R & D staff to get the project done in one or three months. Too often, projects with no deadlines never reach completion. Make it clear that engineers and scientists who complete their projects will get more projects; those who don't, won't.

Turnaround CEOs who do not have a technical background – and most do not – may shy away from hard-nosed assessments of R & D. That's understandable. It's wrong, too. Turnaround CEOs can recruit a senior management team to review all R & D projects: What will each project do for marketing, for operations, for finance? How much do they value the projects? Are they prepared to pay for those projects out of their budgets? If the marketing, operations or finance senior managers do not believe in the project enough to pay for it and if project managers cannot make a convincing argument that the project will support the Turnaround CEO's strategic vision, there is no alternative to immediate cancellation. Re-assign R & D personnel whenever possible; good people are hard to find, and during the later stages of the turnaround as the company prepares for growth, those highly skilled people will be needed. A year in sales or manufacturing will be a good education for many R & D people and for their new colleagues. Of course, cash constraints are a consideration; the assigned work must be productive and beneficial to the company.

Products, Processes & Plants: Fix Or Forget It

The same decision-making process applies to products, processes and plants: data gathering, analysis, assessment of whether it needs fixing, can be fixed and is worthwhile to fix, and implementation. The scope and scale may be greater in the case of a plant than a product but the decision-making process is the same. The challenge during the early stages of a turnaround is finding the time to do the data gathering, analysis and assessment. Triage may be the only practical answer. Products, processes and plants should be divided in three – possibly unequal – categories: those that are viable and should be retained and even supported; those that are obviously detrimental at this time to the company; and, those that are not unequivocally good or bad.

The Turnaround CEO should then devote time to those products, processes and plants that are detrimental at this time. Can they be fixed fast – within three months or six months? Are they worth saving? How much will it cost to remediate them? What are the likely financial benefits? Occasionally there will an argument made that a plant will turnaround eventually; the answer is to do a simple present value of the stream of income, with increasingly high discount rates to reflect uncertainty for each future three months or year. If the decision is to try to remediate a problem product, process or plant, a single person must be made responsible for achieving performance benchmarks. If the bench marks are missed in two consecutive quarters, do not adjust the benchmarks; terminate the product, process or plant and, maybe, the person who failed to turn it around. After three - six months, the obviously bad products, processes and plants should have been remediated or terminated. Then, triage should be applied again.

The second triage may use a different criteria: those that are important for long-term success, those that are unimportant or are likely to absorb more resources than they generate or likely to absorb resources better assigned to more important products, processes and plants, and those that are not unequivocally good or bad. This two-step rationalization of operations is fairly common. Turnaround companies may announce one wave of closures and lay-offs and a second wave, usually smaller, in six to eighteen months. It takes that long to collect, analyze and assess pertinent, reliable data, even in small companies where the complexity is much less but the managerial resources are also much less than in large companies.

CASE STUDY: ROOFING EQUIPMENT COMPANY[16]

The Company

This was a small family company. The founder had built the company over many years and was still the major shareholder. He was 70 years old and had some health problems. He was not able to manage the business on a day-to-day basis. His son-in-law who had previously been the purchasing manager for the company was President and General Manager. There was not a board of directors, but there was an advisory board that included the company's accountant and lawyer.

Illustration: Alexandra Astafyeva

Financial performance had deteriorated. The company's bank restricted credit and increased interest rates and fees. The company hired a turnaround consultant on a six-month contract.

The Business's Three Divisions

The company leased its large warehouse and manufacturing facility in north Toronto from the majority shareholder. The business had three parts: a manufacturer of equipment used by commercial and domestic roofers, a distributor of tools and materials used in roofing and a new manufactured product line. 60% of the revenue was from distribution of roofing products and 40% from manufacturing equipment. The new product line was not generating significant revenue.

Economic Environment

In the early 1990s, companies were struggling to adapt to the changing market conditions created by the introduction of the Free Trade Agreement between the United States and Canada (later expanded to include Mexico and renamed the North American Free Trade Agreement). Canadian manufacturing plants and branch plants of American multinational companies were described as having too much variety of products and unable to achieve economies of scale compared to higher volume manufacturing plants in the US. In addition, small, inadequately capitalized Canadian manufacturers did not have the financial resources to expand. Finally, the Canadian dollar was relatively strong, which affected both imports and exports.

Distribution

The company had warehouses across Canada but not in every province. Major inventory was held in Toronto and Montreal with smaller inventories in Vancouver, Winnipeg and Halifax. Each warehouse had a sales manager who spent most of his time managing the warehouse and very little time actually selling. Sales at the smaller warehouses were stagnating as there was little selling effort and margins were slim. Financial pressures due to costs and cash flow squeezed inventories, resulting in poor fill rates and further loss of revenue. The smaller warehouses had poor fill levels and were not achieving the level of sales of fast moving and profitable tools and consumables that they should have been given the market conditions.

Remedial Actions

The priority was to minimize expenditures. This was done by a line-by-line analysis of spending and putting in a purchase order process that was fairly elementary but quick to install and make effective.

Inventories were thoroughly examined and obsolete material was liquidated. Surplus inventory was identified and liquidated to release warehouse space and free up cash for fast moving inventory. The company made plans to close the smaller warehouses. The larger warehouses would ship by common carrier the larger and high value products direct to the customers' premises or the actual construction site. Each salesman in these territories was issued a van fitted to carry an inventory of small tools and consumables. This was not well received by some of the salesmen who had a comfortable life until then, but those who embraced the program made significant increases in sales and remuneration. A new sales incentive program was introduced at the same time.

Manufacturing

Some of the products were very well thought of in the market place. Some major products were over-engineered compared to the competition; those products rarely needed replacement. Manufacturing equipment was old and very labor intensive, having been protected by high import tariffs until the Canada-US Free Trade Agreement. The main attempt to reduce manufacturing cost had been investing in the latest cutting technology which was very efficient at high volumes; however, there was insufficient volume to justify the machine and it stood idle too much of the time. The manufacturing business was losing market share as cheaper products from the US started to penetrate the market; therefore, there was considerable pressure on the pricing of the manufactured products. As volumes dropped, manufacturing overheads were spread over smaller volumes creating a downward spiral in profitability.

Remedial Actions

An immediate priority was examination of the variable costs of the manufactured products. Anything that was not contributing was immediately cancelled. Anything that could be bought in the market place for less than the company's full cost, with overheads applied, was outsourced and in-house production was discontinued. These actions reduced the number of manufactured products by about 50%. Labor associated with discontinued products was laid off. Manufacturing overheads were examined and plans were made to reduce those over time.

New Products

Attempts had been made to diversify the product range. Prototypes of warning signs for road construction or accident sites using the latest technology had been developed. Today this type of equipment is commonplace but in the early 1990s it was very advanced. Initially the consultant thought that the new products would be part of the solution, but the new products ended up becoming part of the problem. Using the latest technologies with engineering staff with relatively limited experience in this field meant that the new products were unreliable and much more expensive compared to the existing, competitive products.

The major marketing issue was that the only large volume purchasers of these products in Canada were the provincial Ministries of Transport. Each Ministry might have been prepared and able to purchase a few prototypes for evaluation; but volume purchases would have required a tender to be issued. There was no way that any Ministry was going to issue tenders unless it was satisfied that the product was reliable and cost effective. Expectations that the new products would sell in volume were constantly being deferred.

Remedial Actions

Improving quality and gaining a profitable sales level were going to be expensive without the quick results that were needed. The company cancelled the development of the road sign as it was clear there was not the expertise in the organization to fix the problems, there was no sales force experienced in selling to governments and there were not the time and resources to fix both issues.

Strategic Options

Option One

One strategic option was to stay in distribution and to become a national distributor for products made anywhere in the world. Several new products were identified, especially from Europe where the environmental issues of building and reconstruction were already being addressed. It was only a matter of time before environmental issues and responsible products became prominent in Canada and the US. To grow distribution would require new non-family management, likely significant time and incurrence of high risk. Another consideration was that the warehouse and manufacturing facility in north Toronto was in an area that was rapidly being developed into residential property. The majority shareholder's ownership of the property was more valuable than his investment in the business.

Option Two

The alternative was to cash out: sell the business and retain the property in the short term and then sell it for redevelopment at the right time. The consultant concluded that an orderly exit was the right decision for the majority shareholder. Given the family circumstances the advisory board recommended the exit strategy. After the turnaround consulting contact was completed the business was sold to a competitor for a reasonable price and the property sold, it was reported, at a significant profit.

Commentary on the case

There are a number of very interesting points in this case. First, the turnaround consulting contract was a six-month contract, and in that time there were major decisions made and largely implemented. Clearly, urgency prevailed.

Second, operational decisions were data-driven: warehouse fill rates, inventory turnover rates, variable manufacturing costs and so on. Capturing the data and converting the raw data into useful information would have required a concerted effort. In fact, operational issues and decisions strongly dominated the turnaround. The decisive actions on warehouse closures, rationalizing the products manufactured and shutting down the diversification into the new products are all impressive.

Third, while the case study does not provide enough information to know, a good guess is that the start of the diversification to new products and the required investment in equipment, engineering talent and sales efforts would have strained the company's financial and managerial resources. Possibly, the diversification effort and investment may have been a major cause of the company's descent into a turnaround position.

Fourth, the people issues and the marketing issues obviously affected several key decisions. The people issues included inexperienced engineers. The issue of the quality of management was not explicitly described; however, a reasonable inference might be that the majority shareholder had promoted a family member who may not have had the training, coaching, experience or, perhaps, aptitude. The decision to exit by selling the business and then selling the real estate may have hinged on the perceived ability of the family member.

Fifth, in this case, once the initial phases of the turnaround were achieved, the owner decided to exit: the improved distribution and manufacturing was sold to a competitor. It is likely that an attempt to sell the business before the successful completion of the early phases would have been at a discounted price.

CHAPTER 9: THE RIVER THAT RUNS THROUGH IT: STRATEGY

As the turnaround progresses, the Turnaround CEO should make time to "Step back, see the unbounded sea and sky." [17] Turnaround companies have compressed time and constrained resources. They do not have the time or resources of large companies in robust financial health to devote considerable resources to long-range strategic planning. Nonetheless, they must have a corporate strategy – even if only weakly expressed or dimly viewed in the early fog of a turnaround. The Turnaround CEO must have a destination to guide his or her navigation. Activity without strategy is a dog chasing its tail: maybe the dog will catch something but more likely it will go around and around in circles. So, take the 'around and around' out of turnarounds. It is better to plan through a fog than to march forward in blindness. The CEO should start to develop a well-articulated strategy to guide the Consolidation of Progress phase. If the Turnaround CEO is an experienced company employee who has been promoted into the driver's seat of a careening car, he or she may have some strong, fresh, innovative ideas on corporate strategy, but a company insider's ideas may be variations on the legacy - 'the same old same old.' If the CEO is freshly recruited from outside the company or outside the industry, he or she may need six to twelve months to develop a coherent strategy.

Common questions that a Turnaround CEO asks early in a turnaround

- What is the core of this company?
- What is this company really good at?
- What do the customers want this company to be really good at?
- What is profitable now and what will be profitable in the long term?
- What is the sustainable competitive advantage now and in the future?
- What do we need to do better, faster, cheaper?
- And, quite commonly, Gezzzzzz, what's not broken?

---

[17] A traditional Chinese folk saying, quoted by Dai Lin, a Chinese mechanical engineer.

The Tactical Strategy Clusters

Strategy is about long term, wide impact corporate decisions. Tactics are about short term, narrow impact decisions. In practice, the distinction between strategy and tactics is blurred. The Turnaround CEO should be comprehensive in considering the clusters of related issues lurking in the shadows of an uncertain future.

Shareholders & management issues

Prudent Turnaround CEOs identify potential shareholders with goals congruent with the company's goals. A vexing problem arises in turnarounds when current shareholders have conflicting needs and goals. If shareholders have irreconcilable expectations there is often no attractive alternative to the purchase of the dissident shareholder's shares by the dominant shareholder, the company itself or a new, compatible shareholder. Another vexing problem is shareholder / executives who view the company as a lifestyle vehicle rather than a profit-maximizing enterprise.

A pervasive assumption can be that management during the turnaround is a constant for the duration of the planning horizon. An assessment of the turnaround team's capabilities in relation to corporate needs and goals for growth and recovery may be painful; however, avoidance of a frank assessment can lead to strategic choices unsupported by managerial resources. The worst scenario is keeping entrenched management that is unsuited to the company's challenges.

Risk tolerance is fundamental to shareholder and management expectations and decision-making. Business involves risks, but the risks should be consistent with risk tolerances (and rewards).

Company self-image & attitudes issues

All companies need to be marketing oriented, but not all companies should be marketing dominant. Some companies should be operations dominant. Generally, the more specialized a company's assets and personnel, the more dominant operations should be.

A company's attitude to its industry will be shaped by its industry's competitiveness. A company may make a decision to become aggressive, adopt defensive tactics, adopt a conciliatory stance or follow a path of abandonment of customer or product niches to stronger or more aggressive competitors. Avoidance of harshly competitive niches may be an astute choice during a turnaround.

Focus means an exclusive or near exclusive marshaling of financial and human resources on one or a few product or customer categories. Diversification means spreading company resources over several or even many product or customer categories. Focus exposes a company to the reliance on a narrow group of customers and products. Diversification offers the potential of risk spread across multiple categories of customers and products. Many turnaround companies are too diversified and should delete customer and product categories to liberate capital and human resources and re-direct resources to high potential customer and product niches.

Financial performance issues

In the early stages of a turnaround, achieving profits sufficient to service debts is the simple, stark goal. Later, Return On Equity and secondary financial metrics become corporate goals. A note of caution: Using only a financial goal line is dangerous; financial measurements should be used in conjunction with measurements of customer retention and satisfaction, product excellence, employee training and satisfaction, and adherence to environmental, health and safety and employment standards.

The decision to be revenue driven or cost driven has many implications for capital expenditures, marketing programs, staff recruitment and training and even administrative controls. Growth has appeal and dangers. Rapid growth places tremendous strain on management and staff: the skills, policies and procedures suitable previously may be stretched to inadequacy. Moderate growth may stretch but not fracture a company's current and available human and financial resources. Detailed financial projections should indicate the maximum, safe pace of finance-able growth. Despite its allure, growth may not be the best strategy. Shrinking the company can be a legitimate strategy. Asset accumulation is sometimes determined by the availability of capital. Conversely, assets may drive strategy if assets cannot be readily re-directed to new products or customers, transformed to new uses or sold at a price that would be more profitable than continued use. The company should plan its proportionate mix of debt and equity, use of patient capital from pension funds, less patient venture capital or bank debt, the mix of short and long term debt, the mix of floating and fixed interest rate debt, debt denominated in two or more currencies and, perhaps, various hedges.

Customer issues

A company's view of customers is fundamental to its customer strategy. The best view of customers is that customers are one third of a transaction chain extending from the company's suppliers through the company itself to the customer. This view suggests that none of the participants could exist without the other two, that there is an economic value created for each of the three participants in the chain and that gains can accrue to the company by economically creating value for customers. The company - customer relationship is about creating value and allocating the value through the price of the goods and services transferred forward from the company. A different and often correct view is that the company and its suppliers and customers are adversaries, which indicates different strategies and tactics.

Product issues

Companies may reasonably choose either low cost or high differentiation; however, to be successful, companies must align all facets of operations, marketing and administration to the strategy. The ultimate low cost company would be a coalmine. The ultimate high differentiation company would be a contractor building a cathedral. Turnaround companies may be half big, meaning that they incur substantial costs without the benefits of scale. Or, they become half flexible, meaning they suffer from somewhat inflexible manufacturing equipment and processes without the benefits of scope. A key decision is to move operations gradually closer and closer to the optimum configuration.

Innovation & technology

Companies must innovate or become obsolete. Thousands of small innovations might be within the budgets of turnaround companies. New advertising media, alternate employee reward systems and benefits, continuous improvement of manufacturing processes and new products and product features may be considered. Late adoption of innovation (by which time the innovation is no longer innovative) may be inadequate to restore competitiveness.

People issues

Strategy should determine employees. Employees who do not fit the strategy need to be retrained or fired (in a humane manner). Selecting a corporate strategy to 'keep our people busy' shows a lack of knowledge of the demands of the competitive environment and a managerial aversion to tough choices.

The cultural and organizational choice is between rigidity and fluidity. Rigidity is clear rules, firm job descriptions and hierarchical reporting arrangements. Fluidity is shared values guiding daily actions, employee commitment and group responsibilities. Rigidity may be entirely appropriate when the consequences of mistakes are high (hospital operating rooms and bank commercial lending departments) and in highly regulated industries (abattoirs) and repetitive work environments (brick laying). The choice of positioning along the continuum between total rigidity and total fluidity may be nudged a bit by managerial preferences.

Change issues

The corporate challenge is to change the things that must be changed (and can be changed) to achieve congruence with the evolving world. So many things are broken even at the half way point in a turnaround that stability or a leisurely pace of change are likely to be ineffective; however, adjusting in small increments can be effective in the later stages of a successful turnaround. Rapid transformational change offers the appeal of large potential benefits and the dangers of unanticipated consequences that weaken the company's core strengths. In the early phases of a turnaround, accelerated speed may be the only viable approach. In the later phases of a turnaround, staff will be fatigued, angry and resistant to continued, accelerated change; a slower speed of change may be advisable – which is an additional argument for fast change early in the process.

Screening To The Core

Many ideas and options may be developed during the early phases of a turnaround; the Turnaround CEO must screen out those ideas and options that do not pass a series of tests.

Tests to screen ideas and options

- Common sense: Managerial judgment is the first screen. Does it smell right? Does it make good intuitive sense, if the resources (money, people, technology) were available?
- Special pleadings: A department or product group may argue that its case is special, that the company must have a particular activity or product because the customer wants it (but may not pay enough to make it profitable). Family businesses are vulnerable to special pleadings by family members seeking to justify their corporate existence. Any argument that does not persuasively state the benefit to the company is probably a special pleading.
- Life support for yesterday's failures: Many managers will not accept that apparently good ideas failed. The pertinent question is: knowing what we know now, would we invest in this product, service or activity?
- Simplification principle: Some ideas may be valid but overly complex as formulated. Break down the overly complex into clear, complete components. Assess each idea, activity or program on the basis of the company's future ability to implement successfully.
- Non-core: The non-core activity drains money and talent. What actions are to be taken to end non-core activities and to sell non-core assets?
- Power of the collective: Ideas that individually have little impact may collectively have the power to transform the company. Knit small ideas into a meaningful benefit.

- Meaningful benefit: Everything takes time, talent and money. Delete even inexpensive or easy activities or programs if their potential benefit is not meaningful, unless the collective benefit is significant.
- Adequacy of financial resources: Delete ideas that are too expensive under any reasonably feasible conditions.
- Adequacy of human resources: Ideas that require new employees or new skills should be carefully considered in light of the company's ability to hire the people or develop the skills.
- Unacceptably high risk: Risks include financial risk, market acceptance risk, dependency (on a customer or supplier) risk, staff risk and technology risk.
- Unintended consequences: Unintended consequences happen when the natural linkages of financial flows and relations between people, suppliers and customers are forgotten. A useful technique for searching for unintended consequences is to ask what the mid- and long- term impact would be on each of the paradigms.

Priorities & Implementation

Determine the relative importance of actions or issues. Certain judgments are unavoidably subjective: the adaptability of corporate culture, the capacity of senior management to grow in sophistication as the business grows, the vulnerability of current products to technical obsolescence. Objective criteria are relevant: Return On Equity, working capital, cash flow, debt servicing coverage, cyclicality of demand, manufacturing defect rates and environmental protection costs. Ranking priorities may be by intuition or a numeric method. A numeric method forces greater rationality and may build consensus in the senior management team. Implementation is the real test of a successful plan. Consider the managerial effort that will be required to successfully implement the plan. What will be the impediments, the allies, the enemies and the passive resisters? What is the communications plan specific to each stakeholder or stakeholder group?

CHAPTER 10: SHUFFLING THE DECK: FINANCIAL RESTRUCTURING [18]

This overview of restructuring is not a definitive guide or legal or regulatory advice. A more detailed review is contained in Chapters 5, 11, 12, and 14 - 17 of "Corporate Finance For Canadian Executives" edited by Howard E. Johnson (Thomson-Carswell Publishing: Toronto, 2007). Professional advice from an insolvency lawyer, a trustee in bankruptcy or other professional qualified to provide advice in your country is essential. Legal advice on directors' liabilities is advisable.

Strategies for dealing with the creditors during a turnaround range from proposals to creditors, either informally or under bankruptcy laws, sale of the business and receivership or bankruptcy. The top priority of most restructurings is to improve liquidity. If you have no cash and have reached the maximum on your lines of credit, you may have no future. Debt restructuring is a process that allows a company under financial hardship to reduce and renegotiate its debt. The objective is to improve liquidity and reduce leverage (debt) so that the company can continue its operations. The turnaround professional will seek to understand the cash requirements of the business by preparing detailed short-term and longer-term forecasts, including the requirements for ongoing capital expenditures to maintain operations, debt servicing requirements and any unusual items that will impact liquidity. Current financial records are essential to prepare proper forecasts. Restructurings are preferable to bankruptcies as they are less disruptive and damaging to the business, can be completed quickly (with the co-operation of creditors) and may be less expensive.

---

[18] © Brian K. Hunter

Valuation Of A Distressed Business

Before considering proposals to creditors or a sale, consider the value of the business. Be realistic about the value. The most commonly used methods of valuation are the multiple of earnings, discounted cash flow and asset value methods; however, valuing a distressed business can be difficult in that traditional methods may not apply if that the business does not have a history of earnings.

The multiple of earnings approach can be used to quickly value a company. Calculate sustainable EBDITA (Earnings Before Depreciation, Interest, Taxes and Amortization), multiply EBITDA by the appropriate multiple for the industry, and then add or deduct an amount for balance sheet items such as excess working capital. To calculate sustainable EBDITA, adjust for extraordinary items and other costs that will not be borne in future by the purchaser, such as excessive management compensation and bonuses, losses incurred on discontinued operations or products, and gains or losses on the sale of fixed assets.

Most business valuators employ the discounted cash flow approach. Prepare a detailed long-term cash flow forecast, excluding interest expenses, and then apply an appropriate discount rate to arrive at a net present value. This method incorporates assumptions about factors that may impact future cash flow; for example, additional revenues from a plant expansion to be completed next year would be factored into the forecast.

If there are no historical or forecast earnings, an asset valuation may be appropriate. An asset valuation will normally be lower than the other two methods as no goodwill will be attributed. Real estate and equipment are appraised on a going concern / value in use basis. If the business has or will shortly cease operations then an orderly liquidation or forced sale (auction) value is more appropriate.

The standard definition of fair market value is: "the highest price obtainable, in an open and unrestricted market, between informed parties, neither party being under any compulsion to transact, acting at arms length, expressed in terms of cash". Rarely would a distressed business be sold under those circumstances. Expect that the purchase price will be impacted if the business is being sold under duress, if inadequate information is available to the purchaser, or if the purchaser has inadequate time to complete normal due diligence. Your calculation of fair market value should be used only as a guide.

Intangible assets that may offer hidden value

- Brand names
- Patents and trademarks
- Proprietary products
- Undervalued real estate and prime locations
- Long term leases at below market rates
- Tax loss carry forwards
- Skilled workforce
- Distribution rights
- Advantageous supplier or customer contracts.

Informal Debt Restructurings

A comprehensive debt restructuring will deal with each class of liability. The first liability to consider is bank debt. In severe situations the bank may have issued a letter of default; there may have been a forbearance agreement negotiated to enable the borrower to continue to operate under very restrictive terms and conditions for a specified time; and the bank will likely try to ratchet down the availability under the line of credit. In situations such as this, it is often best to consider refinancing the bank debt by moving to an asset based lender ("ABL"). ABLs tend to be much more flexible in distress situations. They look to their collateral security to determine lending values, not the operating cash flows of the business, and they often impose fewer covenants. Often they can provide a higher margining formula for accounts receivables and inventory, thereby enabling the company to access more credit. In conjunction with switching to an ABL, the company should consider the possibility of raising additional long-term debt or equity to reduce short-term borrowings.

Renegotiating credit terms with trade suppliers is commonly used to improve liquidity. It may be possible to freeze the current accounts payable by agreeing to pay COD for future purchases. Suppliers have a vested interest in seeing you succeed; by cooperating they stand a greater chance of getting paid and retaining a long-term customer. Negotiations with suppliers will be more successful if the company can promise additional purchase volumes, either from future growth or from consolidating purchases with the most cooperative suppliers.

Customers may agree to supply raw materials to complete their order. This would reduce purchases and accounts payable. Some customers will also agree to faster payment terms. Some customers will provide advance payment terms to a company that is a sole source supplier of a product not easily acquired elsewhere.

Existing long-term lenders should be approached to see if additional debt is available or if repayment terms may be altered. Many term lenders will consider a deferral of principal payments during a restructuring period. If the lender faces a substantial risk of loss, it may defer or reduce interest or even convert debt to equity.

A sale / leaseback strategy is occasionally used to improve the balance sheet. For example, a trucking company with four-year-old tractors and trailers, which were financed by a five-year term loan, could sell the equipment and use the proceeds of sale to pay off the term loan and any remaining funds to reduce the line of credit or trade payables. Simultaneously, the trucking company could obtain 100% financing of new trucks and trailers with off-balance sheet operating leases. The end result is an improved working capital ratio and a lower debt to equity ratio. Also, any gain on the sale of fixed assets would improve retained earnings.

Companies with a low debt to enterprise value may be able to arrange a layer of subordinated or mezzanine debt. Subordinated and mezzanine debt ranks below the secured creditors but ahead of shareholders, and it normally carries an interest rate 5% to 15% above prevailing bank rates and may include options on shares as a sweetener. The lender will impose a number of restrictive financial covenants covering the working capital ratio, debt to equity ratio, debt service coverage and restrictions on capital expenditures, dividends, investments and voting control. While this is a more expensive form of debt, it is usually cheaper than equity and the owners continue to have free rein subject to satisfying the lender's covenants.

If more debt is not appropriate, it may be possible to arrange additional equity in the form of common or preferred shares. The new investor will likely require a seat on the board of directors and will closely monitor management's progress in implementing the turnaround strategy. Expect active intervention if targets are not achieved. Few institutional investors will take an equity stake in a turnaround. Strategic investors (supplier, customer or competitor) or angel investors (family, friends or mentor) may be more likely investors in a turnaround.

In dire situations it may be necessary to make a structured but informal proposal to creditors. The company could offer trade creditors immediate payment of "X" cents on the dollar currently owing. This would be financed by a new equity or debt injection conditional on the support of the creditors. Some creditors will be inclined to take a discount if they believe that the company would fail without this informal restructuring. This is best handled by an experienced insolvency professional.

Formal Debt Restructurings

In Canada business insolvencies are covered under the Bankruptcy and Insolvency Act ("BIA") and the Company Creditors Arrangement Act ("CCAA"), and most economically developed countries have similar legislation. Typically, a company files with the Court a notice of intention to file a proposal under the BIA because it is unable to raise further financing and is under extreme pressure from creditors. This filing with the Court provides the company with a 30-day stay of proceedings which prevents current creditors from acting on their security and prohibits the company from making payments to its current creditors as of the date of filing. This stops the bleeding. The company may continue to operate during the stay period and negotiate with creditors. If necessary the company can go back to the Court and obtain extensions of the stay for up to five further months. However, if no proposal is filed by the expiry of the stay period, the company is deemed bankrupt.

Creditors have the right to appeal to the Court if they believe that the company is not acting in good faith or if the company is unlikely to make a viable proposal. The proposal to the Court must deal with all unsecured creditors and usually deals with the secured creditors as well. All creditors have the opportunity to vote by class on the proposal. A two-thirds majority must be obtained. Often proposals provide for the full repayment of small creditors, say under $1,000, to ensure that the proposal will pass. If the proposal is not approved, the company is deemed bankrupt.

Once a proposal in bankruptcy has been made it may be possible to continue operations of the business by arranging Debtor in Possession ("DIP") financing. Having a DIP financing facility improves the likelihood that ongoing suppliers will be paid. The company may be able to resume near normal payment terms with suppliers during the stay of proceedings period. The Court will grant the DIP lender a security interest in the company's assets in priority to the existing creditors. The DIP lender could be an existing lender to the business, such as a chartered bank, or an external lender that specializes in this type of funding. It is usually faster and more convenient to use an existing lender that understands the business; however if the relationship between the company and its lenders has turned adversarial, the company may seek an external DIP lender. DIP lenders earn high fees and charge higher interest rates than traditional lenders.

For larger companies with debts in excess of $5 million, an alternative to filing under the BIA is to file under the CCAA. The advantage of filing under the CCAA is that there is no limit on the number or length of extensions of the stay of proceedings. The company normally negotiates DIP financing to fund ongoing operations during the stay of proceedings period, and then files an application to the Court for approval of financing at the time of application for protection under the CCAA. Most large public companies choose the CCAA route to accomplish their very complicated restructurings. Courts will normally approve an Administrative Charge as well, which provides a first charge over the assets of the company in priority to the DIP lender and existing creditors in order to secure the services of professionals such as lawyers, accountants and turnaround consultants retained by the company to effect the restructuring. On large CCAA files, the administrative charge can run into the millions of dollars. BIA filings are normally less expensive. Having obtained the stay, the company must formulate a plan to restructure its debts and continue operations. Alternatively, it may choose to sell the business in order to maximize the value of the business and minimize directors' liabilities.

Sale Of Business By Shareholders

If the company has not been able to complete a debt restructuring, a sale of the business while it remains a going concern or a sale of certain assets or a division may be an option. A sale will require consent of the secured creditors, and the transaction must qualify under the Bulk Sales Act, which prevents business owners from secretly transferring their assets to another company to avoid paying creditors. An experienced business professional should be hired to conduct the sale process.

A quick sale process adds risk as purchasers may not have time to complete all their due diligence. The purchaser may offer a discounted price to compensate for the potential risks and complications of purchasing an insolvent or near-insolvent company. Also, the purchaser will likely consider that the representations and warranties provided by the vendor to have little financial value.

Be prepared to provide some vendor financing if the purchase price includes some value for goodwill. Vendor notes are typically repaid with interest over a three to five year period; security is normally subordinate to all other secured creditors, and often the vendor must standstill for a period of time if the secured creditors' loans go into default.

Strategies to maximize the sale price and pace

- Prepare a consistent explanation of why the business is for sale, which emphasizes the strengths of the business, its competitive advantage and future opportunities available to new owners.
- Clean up the plant. Often repairs and maintenance have been neglected.
- Get rid of redundant assets. The buyer doesn't want the vacation condo or the company airplane.
- Eliminate money losing operations and products. The losses can then be treated as non-recurring and normalized earnings can be upwardly adjusted.
- Submit your tax refund claims for scientific research, excise taxes and so on.
- Resolve outstanding litigation, warranty claims, and customer and supplier disputes.
- Ensure key staff will remain during the sale process. You may have to offer incentives.
- Prepare a "data room" with accurate and detailed records readily available.
- Eliminate excess employees prior to the sale, as new owners don't want to deal with them.

<u>Sale by shareholders under CCAA or BIA</u>

A company may convince creditors to allow management to continue to run the business and manage the sale process, under the supervision of a Trustee in Bankruptcy or Receiver, by pointing out the creditors' potential exposures to risks. These risks may include environmental claims, successor employer claims, product liability claims and pension claims. For creditors to agree, management must have the trust and confidence of creditors; otherwise, creditors may refuse and a Receiver, Receiver-Manager or Trustee in Bankruptcy will be responsible for any sale. After the company signs an agreement with a buyer it will then make a proposal to creditors on the distribution of funds to each class of creditors. Creditors will be given notice of the proposal and an opportunity to raise objections with the Court. The company will still need to satisfy the Court that the recommended offer is the best overall offer and that the sale process was conducted fairly. Typically, a competitive sale process, such as publishing a notice of sale with request for bids within a short time period, is necessary to convince the Court and the creditors. This is especially important if creditors are not being repaid in full. If the creditors vote down the company's proposal it will be placed in bankruptcy.

The sale of a business under a bankruptcy proposal is a complicated transaction; business owners should have professional assistance from advisors experienced in preparing and negotiating proposals to creditors and conveying assets of insolvent companies.

Bankruptcy Or Receivership

If attempts to restructure or sell the business fail, the company may find itself in receivership or bankruptcy. At that point there is typically no financial value to shareholder equity and likely insufficient resources to pay creditors in full. Accordingly, creditors will look after their interests first: minimize their losses and recover their funds as soon as possible.

A sale under receivership or bankruptcy will likely diminish the value of the business as it will now be sold on an "as is, where is" basis, with very limited or no warranties and recourse. In some cases, the highest offer is not the winning bid; the Receiver or Trustee will show preference to buyers that offer all cash, that are able to close the deal quickly and that have the fewest conditions that might upset a sale. Timing and closing risks are critical as the value of a business can quickly diminish if customers, suppliers and employees begin to leave.

The purchaser will require a court's vesting order and approval of the sale. The court's vesting order provides that on completion of the sale, the purchaser owns the purchased assets free and clear of all claims, liens and encumbrances. Receivers and Trustees in Bankruptcy take directions from the Court (not the shareholders or creditors) and therefore no meeting of creditors is required to approve a sale. The Court will determine the distribution of funds. All creditors will be given notice and an opportunity to raise objections.

CHAPTER 11: BRAINS, GUTS & STAMINA

In a turnaround shareholders, staff, creditors, suppliers, regulators and the media may have unreasonable expectations that the Turnaround CEO has the magic medicine to spread on the jagged corporate wound. The Turnaround CEO must make wise choices under conditions of stress, time pressures, inadequate information and uncertainty of outcome. Usually, time is short – bankers are on the phone daily, customers are complaining, and staff morale may be about as high as the spirits of an allergy sufferer in ragwood season. It's tough. Brains, guts and stamina are essential. Secondary characteristics include industry knowledge, high numeracy, financial savvy, ruthlessness, non-clinical obsessive-compulsive behavior, hardiness and 'thick-skinned-ness'. Charm or even charisma would be a bonus. But, the big three are brains, guts and stamina. Commonly, Turnaround CEOs are accused of being obsessive, ruthless, tough, inhumane, bullies and socially unpleasant. Often those are legitimate criticisms. It is a rare individual who can be a successful Turnaround CEO and be loved by those who endure a turnaround.

Brains

Functional background

Most turnarounds are led by finance and marketing people. In the early phases of a turnaround, when cost cutting and persuasion of banks, investors and suppliers are urgent, finance and marketing skills are important and the Turnaround CEO should either have those skills or be supported by staff or a consultant with those skills. As a turnaround progresses to the Consolidation of Progress phase, a broader perspective encompassing all of the paradigms becomes increasingly important. A Turnaround CEO should have general management knowledge, expertise in one of finance, marketing and operations and at least good awareness of the other two functional areas, turnaround skills and a willingness to learn and adjust during the turnaround. However, some turnarounds are led by lawyers and one might expect more lawyers as Turnaround CEOs of large companies with complex contractual arrangements with stakeholders and complicated bankruptcy filings.

Setting priorities

Key decisions must be made fast. The first decision is obvious but often ignored: What three things need to be corrected fast and can be corrected fast? All else must be pushed aside, at least for the day or the week or the month. It may be tempting to make a grocery list of soups and nuts and bread and bananas – all the things that it would be nice to do. But, the priority list during a turnaround must be a maximum of three key priorities – everything else waits. Even very smart people must have a focus, although that focus will almost always evolve during the turnaround.

Selective perception

Determining the priorities takes brains - and wisdom and knowledge. Selective perception is important. The Turnaround CEO must have 'policeman's eyes' – eyes that sweep the streetscape to see danger and spot problems. An experienced person has an intuitive pattern-recognition and a filter that deletes all that is not germane.

Analysis & synthesis

Analytical ability is another component of brains, and the Turnaround CEO must be analytical enough to digest staff reports or to specify the framework for staff to use in data gathering and analysis. Synthesis is the integration of viewpoints and information to create a coherent assessment and vision. The Turnaround CEO may be surrounded by accountants, engineers, lawyers, and marketers, each of whom will have his or her own viewpoint and bias. Only the Turnaround CEO will have the authority and, hopefully, ability to synthesize all of these points of view. If the Turnaround CEO does not have the ability to synthesize he or she will be pulled every which way creating staff confusion and uncertainty at a time when direction and cohesion are vital.

Guts

Most senior management teams have several members who are smart enough to identify good decisions. Brains are not in short supply (usually). However, few senior managers can make tough decisions – they know the answers but they cannot face the unpleasantness of decision-making and implementation. They want to be liked more than they want to be effective. Turnaround CEOs would rather be effective than liked.

Example #1

This example is taken from a real-life situation – and every Turnaround CEO has seen variations of this situation many times. You have reviewed your largest single customer and the data is in the chart below. The customer has told your sales manager that it will change suppliers if you raise prices any amount or if you insist on faster account receivable terms. Your sales manager is strongly against raising prices to this customer. Your HR manager and your sales manager believe that losing your biggest account will destroy employee morale and ruin your company's reputation in the market place. The purchasing manager claims that the volume due to the largest single customer gives your company the ability to achieve volume discounts from suppliers, but she cannot give any figures – even estimates – of how much more your company will pay for inputs if it loses the account. The controller talks about the intangible value of good employee morale and market share. If you raise prices and lose the account, almost a certainty, you will have a disgruntled management team who will resent your arbitrariness. What do you do?

	Largest Customer	**Other Customers**
Sales	27% of total company sales.	2nd largest customer is 9%. Average is 0.9%.
Contribution margin to overhead and profit	0%	20%
Account receivable	70 days	45 days

Example #2

Every Turnaround CEO has seen variations of this situation. Harry is the VP of Warehouse and Logistics Operations – a good family man, 53 years old, started with the company when he was 19 years old, after high school, worked in the warehouse and, as the company grew, he took on more and more responsibility. You think that there may be efficiencies equal to about 2 -3 % of sales, and that some material handling equipment and vehicles could be sold if the efficiencies are achieved. The company is currently losing 4% of sales, and so the potential savings could be a major contributor to a financial recovery. You have discussed your ideas with Harry several times. Each time he becomes angry and insists that his area is in great shape and that there is no way that any improvements could be made. You offer to work with Harry to analyze his area, and Harry becomes angry and resentful. You know, however, that he is popular and, with 34 years' experience with the company, that he has influence within the company. So, what do you do?

Example #3

Another common experience is dealing with lenders. Janice Orsini of Global Bank meets with you and the controller; she is explicit that Global Bank will require a much higher interest rate on all advances and a monthly administration fee (almost equivalent to a full-time salary at Global Bank). Orsini does not quite say that Global Bank will start bankruptcy proceedings if you do not agree, but the threat is implied. The increase in financial costs will postpone achieving breakeven by at least three months and will place a further strain on cash flow. You know that Global Bank is making your bad situation worse and that Global Bank doesn't care. So, what do you do?

Those are three common situations – in each of the situations, the Turnaround CEO must make a decision based on the near-term, the mid-term and the long-term best interests of the company. Meanwhile, there is an innate desire is to preserve interpersonal harmony. In the example of meeting with the banker, the Turnaround CEO must make a decision in front of a staff member, which puts an additional input into the decision-making. Other situations could be imagined: announcing a plant closure, suffering an environmental or public safety debacle and facing a firestorm of media coverage, or confronting unrealistic expectations in union negotiations. These are common, real, highly stressful situations. Few people have the guts to face them and to make the right decisions.

Stamina

How long does it take to turnaround a company? Let's say the company is a manufacturer and it has sales of $50,000,000 and 150 employees and 1,500 customers. It is currently losing customers due to slightly lower quality imports from India. The imports are 15% cheaper. The company is at breakeven and is forecasting a loss of $1,500,000 next year. The process of restoring this failing company to sustainable competitive vitality might be completed in 2 years, but 3 years to adjust products, processes and plants, to re-price accounts, possibly to make changes to the channels of distribution and to revitalize the management team may be more realistic

The Turnaround CEO will be working 50 to 70 hours / week, under a lot of stress including interpersonal stress with lenders, suppliers, customers and staff. Bad news will cascade during the first six months. After six months the bad news may be less frequent but it will be random, so the Turnaround CEO will never be able to relax. There will be progress but there will be setbacks and frustrations. In the first twelve months it will be difficult to take more than a few days' holidays; there is too much to do and senior staff may not be good enough to leave unattended. The turnaround environment is brutal and only those hardy executives who thrive on the adrenalin rush can cope.

But, even hardy executives incur physical and psychological risks associated with prolonged stress and adrenalin stimulation. Risks include heart damage and heart attacks, and social and psychological trauma – battle fatigue. Eventually physical and psychological health and executive decision-making will suffer.

To survive and prosper the Turnaround CEO must have tremendous stamina. Ideally, he or she should also have an engrossing hobby or interest – golf or cross word puzzles or grandchildren. Ideally, he or she should commit to taking mini-holidays of three or four day long weekends three or four times in the first year, and probably taking at least ten days totally away from the company – except in the direst emergency – within 18 months. Ideally, the Turnaround CEO must have at least one person he or she can really trust; and, that is a good reason to hire a former associate to work in the turnaround company in a meaningful role. It is important to have someone to talk with and someone who will speak forthrightly to the Turnaround CEO. Ideally, the Turnaround CEO will have a warm, loving relationship with his or her spouse or significant other.

Groom A Successor

Identify one person or a senior management team who can operate the company for short periods sufficient to allow the Turnaround CEO to take short holidays during the early stages of a turnaround. There is a downside: personnel may have known at the beginning of the turnaround that the change, pain and stress were required to save the company; by the mid-point of the turnaround, people will be drifting to the delusion that sufficient changes have been made and that they really do not need further change, pain and stress. Opposition can coalesce around someone seen as a designated successor. So, the Turnaround CEO should beware of being stabbed in the back.

Epilogue: Buy A Dog

The wise Turnaround CEO gets a dog – the dog will love him or her after the turnaround. Few others will. Staff will have had a highly stressed two or three years; their working lives will have been in turmoil; friends may have been terminated; work patterns and work relationships were likely disrupted; new managers and new expectations were probably imposed. Staff will forget the threats to the survival of the company. Staff will have a strong emotional linkage between the trauma and the Turnaround CEO.

Once the board of directors concludes correctly or incorrectly that the turnaround is done, it may conclude that it does not need the turnaround executive anymore. The board may decide that a new CEO with a growth mandate and a sales orientation is required. The board may decide that the Turnaround CEO has been too expensive and that the salary and bonus cannot be justified in the future. Shareholders may decide that the turnaround was obvious and then want double-digit growth in the future, which is unreasonable in most industries over the mid- and long-term. The wise turnaround executive gets a dog, or moves rapidly into growth mode and solidifies and repairs relationships as soon as it appears that a successful turnaround has been largely achieved.

A Turnaround CEO may also be ejected by conspiracy or ignorance. For example, one battle-weary Turnaround CEO was fired by the board of directors because profits had not rebounded; the Turnaround CEO had advised the board that the industry was in a recession and that profits would soon recover. The board in its wisdom did not become familiar enough with the industry and decided to replace the Turnaround CEO. About three months later the industry and the company rebounded. In that particular case, the chair of the board had the integrity to recognize his mistake and the nobleness of spirit to actively help the CEO - whom he had terminated – to find another high profile job. Boards may only know financial results and may not know or understand that an increase in profits is not conclusive evidence of a successful turnaround; only sustained improvement proves a sustained recovery. Also, boards may not recognize that losses may be the financial lag between action and results. Nonetheless, termination of a Turnaround CEO before a turnaround is really completed does happen.

If the turnaround is not successful, the wise turnaround executive realizes that he or she will be blamed for not saving the company. The board of directors, the unionized workforce, the non-unionized work force, disgruntled suppliers and unco-operative lenders will not look in the mirror the next morning and accept that they contributed to the declining performance of the company and that they did too little, too late to save the company. If the turnaround is not successful, the wise turnaround executive buys two dogs, as he or she will need all the unconditional love available.

The Turnarounders

Turnarounds are done by management. Lenders, lawyers, accountants and consultants may say 'I've done three or twenty three turnarounds.' That's simply not true. They may have recapitalized loans, drafted new contracts or provided other professional services of undoubted value and benefit; but, management runs the company and management does the turnaround.

Take a gunfighter to a gunfight

Turnarounds of mildly distressed companies are pressure packed. Turnarounds of severely distressed companies are chaotic, physically draining, health threatening experiences. The relatively few successful Turnaround CEOs and Turnaround Consultants are hardy, tough individuals who thrive on the adrenaline rush. They are seasoned by prior turnarounds and can remain objective and focused on the ultimate goal of future prosperity and not simply survival during the darkest moments of credit and cash flow crises. The objectivity is especially important: company personnel may be reluctant to accept that divisions must be closed, that product lines must be dropped, that R & D programs must be abandoned and that people must be fired. The focus on the ultimate goal is also important: experienced turnaround professionals know that decisions must balance the consideration of immediate survival with the imperatives of preserving whatever are the company's competitive strengths and assembling the resources required for a recovery.

Turnarounds by existing management without professional assistance

Existing management may do a successful turnaround without professional assistance if all of three conditions are met:

- The cause of corporate distress is a unique, non-recurring event such as a non-insured loss, and
- The company had been operated well and profitably by existing management except for that unique, non-recurring event, and
- The financial losses or lender pressure has not become threatening to the near-term viability of the company.

Otherwise, if the cause of corporate distress is not unique (and it is rarely unique) and if it is recurring (a recession today is likely to be a recession next month and the month after), then existing management may be unwise to attempt a turnaround without professional assistance. Do not expect the management that led the company into the swamp to lead it unassisted out of the swamp.

Turnarounds by existing management with professional assistance

Existing management may do a successful turnaround with professional assistance if all of three conditions are met:

- The existing management has some excellent skills, commitment, work ethic and willingness to learn and implement new ideas and approaches, and
- The turnaround consultant has the experience, skills, toughness and credibility to assist management, and
- Management and the consultant will likely have an effective working relationship based on mutual respect for their respective contributions to a turnaround.

A board's decision to hire a new CEO

Ask any experienced corporate director and he or she will tell you that one of the most difficult board of directors' decisions is whether to replace a CEO. Boards debate whether the CEO is doing well under adverse economic or competitive conditions, if anyone could do better, and if the benefit of a new CEO outweighs the disruption to the company and the costs of severance and the uncertainty of recruitment. There is research that establishes that the tenure of CEOs is becoming less; boards are terminating CEOs faster. Boards may force the hiring of a new CEO if:

- Existing management lacks the skills, commitment or work ethic as demonstrated by how it has operated the company up to the point of a turnaround, or
- Existing management has lost the support of shareholders and lenders, and pressure becomes intense or may likely become intense, and
- The existing CEO does not own a controlling block of shares or have strong friends on the board.

An entrepreneur's decision to hire a consultant or CEO

Anecdotal evidence suggests that entrepreneurs give up leadership and control as readily as drunk drivers relinquish steering wheels. It is a rare and remarkably astute entrepreneur who decides that his or her company's particular situation requires someone to advise him on what to do (a turnaround consultant) or requires someone who will decide what to do and then will do it (a Turnaround CEO). One may argue that entrepreneurs may agree to hiring a turnaround consultant if:

- The entrepreneur recognizes the gravity of the company's situation and the novelty of the situation compared to his or her previous experience and skills, or
- There is great pressure from lenders or, less often, the entrepreneur's spouse, or
- The entrepreneur is experiencing severe stress that causes concern about mental or physical health.

The same factors apply to the hiring of a Turnaround CEO but the factors must be more powerful because the loss of control, prestige and identity is much greater than in the case of hiring a consultant.

Consultants proposed by lenders

Lenders may insist on the hiring of a 'turnaround adviser or consultant', and that in itself is a good idea. However, it is worthwhile to ask what the adviser's background is: the background may be a trustee in bankruptcy or a liquidator. It is worthwhile to ask what the mandate is: the mandate may be to recover the lender's advances, in which case the mid-term survival of the company will not be important to that adviser. The difference between a turnaround consultant and a liquidation consultant is not the name – both are often called management or turnaround consultants. The difference lies deeper. Ask 'what are the loyalties, motives and goals?' If the lender insists on the company hiring a 'consultant' of the lender's selection, insist on written instructions from the lender. There are lenders who act in good faith and do recommend management and turnaround consultants to help companies. Just ask the questions to know the reality of whether the consultant is working for the company or the lender.

Finding, hiring and paying

Large companies may use executive search firms to find candidates for the role of Turnaround CEO and may select one of numerous national and international consultancies as turnaround consultants. Small and mid-sized companies may more likely quietly canvass knowledgeable and discrete lenders, lawyers, accountants, business colleagues and retired executives to identify suitable candidates. The process of hiring is often a process of mutual exploration of strengths, weaknesses and opportunities of both the hiring company and the candidate. Under turnaround conditions, the trepidation may be greater as both the company and the individual will be aware of the risks but neither may be fully aware of the degree of challenge. The candidate will want to build some confidence that the company can be turned around and that he or she will have the independence and support by the board of directors or the owners to make and implement decisions. The board or the owners will want to build some confidence that the candidate possesses the balance of decisiveness and caution that is appropriate to that company's situation.

The cost of a Turnaround CEO or a turnaround consultant will vary with local conditions (major city versus small city), the industry, whether the company is a publicly traded company or privately held, the size of company and the skills and reputation of the candidate and the candidate's alternatives (an executive with a successful company will want to be well paid to leave a safe harbor for a battle zone). Turnaround CEOs may be paid a salary or a salary plus a bonus based on results. Consultants generally are paid on a per hour or per day basis; bonuses are less frequent because the consultant is only an advisor and cannot make decisions or force implementation; therefore, the actual results may not reflect the value offered by the consultant. Consultants' hourly or daily rates are usually about the same as the rates of a good lawyer or accountant.

Occasionally there may have been a mistake in hiring a CEO or consultant, and, like any mistake in hiring, it should be quickly corrected by terminating the relationship and starting a new hiring process. However, one should at least ask if the company itself is the problem (can it be turned around by anybody?), if the board or owners are the problem (has the Turnaround CEO had the independence and support to make decisions and implement, or did the board or owners interfere?) or if action is premature (are there the inevitable lags between analysis and actions on one hand and subsequent, positive results?).

Boards Of Directors

Boards of directors are elected by voting shareholders to govern the company. Directors have significant legal responsibilities and they should receive legal advice on their responsibilities and potential liabilities. Legal advice is especially important because leadership and governance issues and directors' liabilities are far more pressing during a turnaround.

Unfortunately, boards of directors of privately held companies are commonly ineffective. Directors usually have not had direct turnaround experience; they often do not have deep knowledge of the company or industry; and, they are anxious about the reputational and financial risks that they face as directors of a failing company. Shareholders will question the company direction and the directors' decisions, intelligence and work ethic. Directors statutory liabilities for tax remittances, health & safety, environmental damage and general business conduct always exist in theory but in a turnaround the company may not be able to indemnify directors and the turnaround company may be under-performing in regulatory compliance as well as financial performance. The board may receive lots of information from the CEO but the board will not have the intimate knowledge that the CEO has and so the board will not be able to be as confident as the CEO.

Boards of directors commonly wait too long during corporate deterioration before forcing the company into a turnaround mode and, once the company is in turnaround mode, boards commonly have unrealistic expectations of the speed and magnitude of a turnaround and of the potential rapidity of the effectiveness of the Turnaround CEO. The best advice to directors of a turnaround company is, probably, resign. The next best advice is lead, follow or get out of the way. Do not muddle or interfere. Insist on thorough briefings from the Turnaround CEO but be aware that the Turnaround CEO has other stakeholders (lenders, customers, suppliers, staff, unions, regulators, media) whom he or she must satisfy prior to having time to devote to the board's concerns. The Turnaround CEO carries the heaviest load by far; as long as there is reasonable progress as judged on the basis of exogenous and endogenous factors, be supportive.

Directors' two key questions during turnarounds

- Should this company be turned around, or should it be sold or closed?
- If the company should be turned around, who is the best person available and able to turn it around?

Self-Management For The Turnaround CEO

Maintain physical, social & mental health & self-awareness

Maintaining health is so vital that there is a chapter devoted to it. Read it slowly and thoughtfully. Another resource is the website for the magazine, Men's Health. The motto is: 'tons of useful stuff' and while the content is targeted to young and early middle-aged men, it does have 'tons of useful stuff' about nutrition and exercise. http://www.menshealth.com

Awareness of the social environment

Be aware of the social environment. Turnaround CEOs work under a microscope: the board of directors or owners, the senior managers, staff, lenders, suppliers, customers, regulators and, in some cases, media all watch, impute motives and characteristics and pass judgment. Be aware of the scrutiny and be aware that each bit of fatigued body language and scrap of innocent conversation may be interpreted, misinterpreted and mis-communicated. Through all of the working in a fishbowl, be true to yourself, your identity and sense of self-worth, your ethical values and your mental and physical health.

Mega priorities

In the early days of a turnaround, the Turnaround CEO must deal with the short-term crises and at the same time be aware of the long-term. The CEO will do 'triage'. Select the two or three specific issues that are critical to the company's success (e.g.: decrease scrap rate by 12% by January 31). Do something every day to achieve the mega priorities (e.g.: instruct the controller to prepare an update on the inventory status every Friday). Make someone do something every day on the mega priorities. Ask staff what they have done today to reduce inventory or to cut scrap rates. Pay bonuses based on achievement of objectives.

The triage of issues, assets, products and people

- Those that clearly detract from corporate performance and cannot be improved to a satisfactory level in the short-term of 30 days to six months.
- Those that clearly are contributing positively to current performance and will likely contribute positively to long-term performance.
- Those that are not obviously very good or bad – mushy, muddled middle of the road stuff.

Time management

Say no to everything that does not have a meaningful impact on near-term and long-term corporate success. Saying no will delete many unimportant activities and enable a laser-like focus on the mega priorities. Track and analyze the time devoted to mega priorities compared to non-critical tasks. Prepare, update and use a To Accomplish list of items and tasks, responsibilities and deadlines. Take a time management seminar. Get the management team on a shared electronic calendar; there are several available online.

CASE STUDY: CHAIN-LINK FENCING [19]

The Company

The company was established in 1990 as a supplier of chain-link fencing and fence maintenance for commercial, industrial and institutional properties. Two men in their mid-50s owned the company; one was responsible for operations (installation and maintenance) and the second was responsible for sales and administration.

Illustration: Crystal Dai

In 2005 sales were $13,500,000. By 2007 sales had decreased to $9,500,00. In 2006 the net loss was $300,000. In 2007 the net loss was $450,000. By early 2008 the company was at its limit of bank borrowing of $1,800,000 and was out of covenant in all areas of its agreement with its bank. At that point the bank refused to provide continuing support and demanded an action plan within 30 days. The company engaged a consultant.

As always, the immediate priority was to conserve cash. Almost immediately the owners agreed to implement the following steps:

- Salaries to the two owners were terminated.
- Seven employees, out of a total of 37, were terminated immediately.
- All other non-essential expenses were stopped.
- Meetings were held with the four major suppliers.

---

[19] © Fred S. Wagman, 2008.

- All accounts payable were put on hold for 45 days and all future purchases were to be on a COD basis.
- Inventory not required for the next 60 days was returned for credit.

As the consultant's review progressed, it became evident that this business could not successfully continue as currently structured. Demand for the company's products was in a long-term decline. Competition was intense as there were low barriers to entry. Customers typically bought through a public tender process that was price-driven rather than based on quality of installation and after-sales service. These factors caused a relentless squeeze on margins. Declining sales volumes, declining sales margins and minimum levels of overhead and owner remuneration meant that recovery to long-tern profitability was highly questionable. The consultant and the two owners concluded that continuing operations would lead to further losses and that the only available options were to wind the company down, declare bankruptcy or sell the business.

The winding down process would mean that revenues would fall sharply as inventory was sold and new projects did not replace completed projects, margins would fall as the company sold inventory at liquidation prices, and lower gross margins would be inadequate to pay minimum levels of overhead. The losses could be high. The situation might be different for a manufacturer that needed to complete work-in-progress and convert raw materials to finished goods and then to accounts receivable, but for this business winding down would have been very costly and would have severely diminished the owners' equity.

The consultant and the two owners met with an insolvency lawyer to explore options and at the same time they contacted three companies who were in a similar business, two of which were direct competitors. Within three weeks the company and one of its competitors finalized an agreement of purchase and sale, with the transaction to close in 120 days, with appropriate guarantees and assurances from the purchaser. The consultant and the owners were able to satisfy the bank that the planned sale was the most prudent option to protect both the owners' equity and the bank's advances. The bank co-operated on the basis of monitoring its advances until the actual sale transaction. The alternatives of winding down or bankruptcy would have resulted in the owners receiving nothing and yet having significant responsibilities under their personal guarantees held by the bank. Although the owners were unable to recover all of their equity, they did recover at least some equity and they were able to depart from the company without being forced to pay their onerous personal guarantees to the bank.

Commentary on the case study

This is a classic case of rapid, wrenching decision-making during a turnaround. The pressure would have been intense. The case study indicates that after two years of losses and thus increased stress for the owners, the bank issued an ultimatum; by the end of about four weeks the owners had assessed the viability of their business, decided that the future was bleak, decided to sell the business and reached an agreement to sell the business. That's fast.

It's worthwhile to reflect that the bank undoubtedly did not understand the company; but the bank did understand the financial statements and the financial trends. With the active involvement of the turnaround consultant the owners reached the same conclusion that the bank had reached: this company was in the Exit position. In some cases owners may say 'why didn't the bank tell me sooner?' which, of course, is a silly statement given that the owners are responsible for the operations and results of the business. The bank's ultimatum undoubtedly seemed harsh at first; quite possibly, the bank's demand shook the owners out of complacency and saved the owners' remaining equity.

While the case study is silent on the role of the turnaround consultant in helping the owners adjust their assessment of the business and possibly their self-image, turnaround consultants often provide non-clinical psychological intervention to assist strong, committed, dedicated owners to make these adjustments and implement the necessary transitions. (However, there are times that intervention by medical and psychological professionals is highly desirable.)

CHAPTER 12: MENTAL & PHYSICAL HEALTH [20]

The Need To Actively Maintain Health & Functioning

There are two major assumptions that I harbor about turnarounds:

- A turnaround can be dangerous to your health and should be considered a major stressful event because it is negative and usually unanticipated. For that reason, the risk of development of a physical or psychological condition, within a year, is high.
- One should expect that without specific *proactive* attention to one's mental and physical fitness, you are more likely than not to deteriorate to the point of significant loss in your day to day functioning and / or developing an illness (medical or psychiatric).

One needs to understand and accept the importance of taking the measures to optimize your physical and mental health functioning. It is useful to employ the advice advocated by airline attendants to adults traveling with a child on an airplane. That is, in the event of an emergency, apply the mask to yourself first, before attending to the child. Hence, in any turnaround, which is like a long distance run, you won't be able to give yourself a chance to win the race if you are unable to cross the finish line. I think Mohammed Ali referred to surviving a turnaround in boxing, when he noted, even if you take a shot that threatens to turn out your lights, you want to find a way to remain standing to have a chance.

Money and time are two major resources in short supply in a turnaround situation. You are making an investment in buying yourself more time, by keeping yourself in fighting shape and functioning at an optimal level. You are simply trying to prevent *significant* deterioration in your effectiveness / efficiency given the unrelenting demands of a turnaround.

---

[20] © 2008 S. W. Dermer, MD, FRCP(C), Occupational Psychiatric Consultant

Remaining Fit Requires Active Intervention

Being fit requires *active* intervention, as opposed to passively thinking about it or waiting until the crisis is over. Specifically, regular physical and mental activities are recommended, such as, aerobic exercise, stretching, and/or relaxation strategies (i.e. meditation, leisure time activities, etc.). As well, diet must also be managed, including control of caffeine and alcohol intake, while eating a balanced diet and ensuring adequate hydration.

Maintaining Perspective

Many say that you can't consider yourself a businessperson until you have endured a turnaround. It is a truism that almost everyone, sooner or later, in business does eventually have to deal with a turnaround because it's the nature of the beast. This is akin to the successful baseball player who expects to fail to get a base hit two thirds of the time. Nevertheless, given the need for investing our ego in our business, it is often difficult to keep separate the business problem and you as a person (and your self-confidence) – you and the business are not one and the same thing. That is, although you need to care deeply and feel responsible for your business, you and your loved ones are of greater value to you in the long term, than the business irrespective of its problems or successes.

Get Professional Help Early If Needed

How your body and mind are functioning are essentially "canaries in the mine". Significant signs that you may be "leaking oil" or worse, may be one or more of the signs listed in the table below. Aside from physiological warning signs, it is easy to develop a mindset that contributes to slipping backwards. Specifically, you may need to avoid the temptation of punishing yourself by not taking time to be good to yourself. This self-destructive behavior often stems from the belief that, "I created the mess, or I should have prevented it." Alternatively, there is often a need to show others that during the turnaround, you are prepared to "give it your all, even if it kills you." Be prepared to absorb the fears and frustrations of your staff, and even your loved ones, because they may be acting as if you are the root cause of the problem or the solution. This fine balancing act requires you to separate yourself from the problem, without disclaiming responsibility or not caring about solving the problem.

Significant signs (if they are persistent, i.e. two or more weeks)

- Sleep dysregulation (i.e. difficulty falling asleep, frequent awakenings, or early morning awakening).
- Weight loss or gain greater than 5 to 10 pounds over a three-month period or less.
- Mood fluctuations, either too high or too low, irritability, unrelenting pessimism, or panic attacks.
- Sustained loss of energy or interest or significant diminution in pleasure.
- Difficulties with attention, concentration, recall and retention.
- Morbid thoughts and feelings.
- Further definite signs that would prompt you to seek out your family doctor would be significant change in your blood pressure, overwhelming fatigue, palpitations and persistent pain.

Reach Out To Others, And Be Open to Support

Finally, try to keep in mind that in the long term, following on a turnaround, whether you are successful or not, success will largely be measured by you based on how you coped and what you learned. We don't necessarily ask for these challenges, but they often teach us more than our successes.

Be prepared, after resolution of the turnaround (one way or the other) that it may take months to psychologically work through the experience. Along the way, stay in contact with your loved ones (they need you as much as you need them), in addition to taking advantage of outside professional resources who can direct and support you, both during the turnaround and after resolution.

Resources

One good source of information is the book Younger Next Year: Live Strong, Fit, and Sexy--Until You're 80 and Beyond by Chris Crowley, M.D., and Henry S. Lodge; it's available from retail bookstores and online bookstores.

There is a depression checklist at **www.checkupfromtheneckup.ca** and more in-depth information from the Mood Disorders Association at **www.mooddisorders.on.ca**. Those tools are a way of letting business owners give themselves an opportunity to know whether they should be consulting a health professional.

CHAPTER 13: A HUMANISTIC VIEW [21]

"The crisis that sets the context for my study was the Finnish 1990s recession, a recession that between the years 1991 and 1993 caused an economic collapse more serious than had been witnessed by any industrial state since World War II. The great recession that shook our economy may actually only be compared to the situation in those countries hit the severest by the Great Depression of the 1930s. ... During 1991 and 1993 the Finnish GDP shrunk by 12 percent, employment fell by 18 percent and asset prices plummeted. The unemployment rate rose from 3.5 percent in 1990, to 18.4 percent in 1994." Mia Örndahl, Ph.D.

Research On Management And Communication

The thesis I am about to defend is about four companies that survived the extremely severe recession that shook the Finnish economy in the 1990s. My study deals with the companies' crisis handling, focusing on management and communication. Further, I have focused on how the managers and employees I interviewed explained that they managed to remain active and to take control despite the threat of the economic decline situation in the environment. When an organization is struck by crisis, managers may be at loss for what to do next. This will consume much energy desperately needed to keep up business in a situation when the most urgent need is for business to continue. Succeeding in focusing on relevant work and avoiding a state of paralysis in such a situation are major challenges.

I chose to study companies that survived the recession, as I find studying survivors much more of a challenge than studying business failure: it is always easy to point towards what was done wrong. To explore what has been done right, and at the same time accepting that survival is not an outcome only of how the crisis situations were managed

---

[21] © Mia Örndahl, Ph.D.. Doctoral defense, Lectio Praecursoria 24.9.2005.

is a lot more challenging – and more interesting. Add to this elements of luck and coincidence as my interviewees did, and it becomes even more exciting.

When I was a graduate student at the university, there was a 'change, flux and turbulence fad' – each new book about management began stating something like 'in today's turbulent world, nothing is as certain and constant as change.' Change and turbulence had obviously not entered organizational life for the first time in the late 1980s, but on certain levels, changes had increased in business life. Today, we appear to witness an increasing amount of crises of different kinds, and they often occur as a result of something unexpected, or something that could not have been prevented.

Media reports almost on a daily basis of crises in business life, such as crises related to companies downsizing – for instance, after a merger or acquisition, or as a result of economic hardship or in order to avoid potential economic hardship. There are crises caused by strikes, as the case was with the forest industry in Finland last spring. We have seen scandals being revealed, or illegal activities by members of an organization, as in the much discussed Enron case a few years ago.

Crises that cannot or can only with difficulty be predicted and prevented take place, examples of these being crises caused by natural disasters. We recently saw how hurricane Katrina caused a total disruption in the society of the area it hit, and is now followed by hurricane Rita. An extreme example of crises is of course that of acts of terrorism, that obviously have global consequences. There are hence, crises of many kinds on different levels of society that have implications for some or sometimes even most aspects of our lives.

The Finnish recession of 1991 - 1993

Recessions are crises that occur not quite as unexpected and suddenly as for instance an earthquake, but nonetheless lead to organizations dealing with a situation in which the actual cause of the crisis, the recession that shakes society at large, is not something that can be affected by an individual organization. Organizations can only attempt to handle the consequences that the recession has on their everyday life.

The crisis that sets the context for my study was the Finnish 1990s recession, a recession that between the years 1991 and 1993 caused an economic collapse more serious than had been witnessed by any industrial state since World War II. The great recession that shook our economy may actually only be compared to the situation in those countries hit the severest by the Great Depression of the 1930s. Let me refresh your memories by presenting a few facts.

During 1991 and 1993 the Finnish GDP shrunk by 12 percent, employment fell by 18 percent and asset prices plummeted. The unemployment rate rose from 3.5 percent in 1990, to 18.4 percent in 1994. The crisis produced extremely sudden changes, and as a consequence of it Finnish society faced new problems in the 1990s: a realization of a systemic risk in banking; large scale and long-term unemployment and social exclusion; the question of the sustainability of advanced welfare provisions, to name a few. A recession of such a magnitude obviously affects a country in many ways and on many levels of society, and for a long time.

For an organization, such a crisis entails living with an uncertainty that is difficult to imagine during more stable times – it is not merely the case of a disruption in business such as for instance a technical error leading to machines on a factory floor ceasing to function, or a fire that can be extinguished and the consequences dealt with in a more or less clear-cut manner. For situations like these that are not unthinkable it is even possible to prepare manuals. A recession on the other hand, causes a situation in which it is impossible to know how long the crisis will last and how much it will cost the organization. This is the reality the four companies that I studied had to deal with.

It is, then fair to say that the recession being so severe created a state of panic in society, whereby the crisis was experienced as very real, although all four companies included in my study were not directly threatened by bankruptcy. On the other hand, the fact that there was a recession causing the crises in the companies, that threatened business life at large, did make it easier to cope with the situation in the sense that the organizations and their managers were not the ones to blame for the crisis.

The complexity of crises

Organizational crisis management is not an unexplored area of research. It has been studied extensively, the attempt often being to identify causal relationships.

When I started conducting this study, I believed it was possible to come up with, if not causal relationships, then something at least somewhat normative, even to find some new aspect of 'truth' that had not been discovered before. However, I soon realized that what we learn from successful handling of a crisis in one company is not easily transferred as a solution to another company's crisis – the context of surviving a recession is not specific enough to make it possible. Knowledge, and lessons about surviving a recession in one company, then, have to be translated, not transferred, into a local context, as each company differs from the next in its hierarchical structure, culture, way of conducting business and market position, to name a few. An interviewee in my study actually used the metaphor of project management to explain how crises should be handled. He claimed that each crisis is a project that requires the right and relevant constellations of strategies, goals, implementation and people. Quick fix recipes do not exist, I was told by the managers I interviewed.

As I realized how complex the things I was looking at were, my research became more of a project of understanding what happens in crises. This is the reason for my choice of theoretical frame and methodology: that is, social constructionism and a narrative approach. I deliberately chose not to try and point towards a few factors that appear to be causally linked to survival, I wanted to try and grasp a broader picture, to understand, and contribute to a lack of understanding that I perceived to exist. This was rewarding in the sense that I could go out in the field not asking for replies to ready made questions, but for explanations to help me understand.

However extensively changes and crises have been addressed and studied, even with increasing urgency, we still have much to learn about the social and human side of organizational crisis situations – that is, in relation to questions such as what happens when we find ourselves in a crisis situation? How do we deal with it? And, most importantly: How can we learn to handle and deal with crises more successfully in order to decrease unnecessary failure, losses and suffering?

A former CEO with vast experience as a manager of companies in crisis recently stated to me that our Finnish management culture needs more than numbers, as human beings are the ones who carry out the work. For this very reason it is important to understand the dynamic character of how we make sense of what happens, and how we interpret social interactions, and even: how we act upon our own interpretations of the social world.

Individuals As Actors In Companies

One way of gaining this understanding is through collecting stories. Through telling stories we construct our own versions of what happened. The stories we tell are influenced by social contexts, and by social relationships, as well as by our own motives. I argue that we tend to claim to be more rational than we are and to behave more logically than we do, and through the explanations and rationalizations that the stories we tell consist of, we justify our not so rational behavior, and make it sound more sensible.

This, however, does not mean that the stories that we tell, or the stories my interviewees told me are not true: their stories about what happened are rationalizations, yes, but social life consists of constant interpretations of what happens around us. If we fail to take into consideration the interpretations based upon which people act and react, we are left with only a small part of the picture.

Studying what happened in the past is as important as conducting studies during the recession, as well as immediately after. Stories told in hindsight of how a crisis was experienced means that some distance has been put between the events and the present time. This allows for less emotionally charged evaluations of what happened, perhaps seeing some things more 'clearly', if you wish. Talking about a crisis after a number of years may lead to completely new and highly valuable aspects being revealed, as new experiences help shape and make sense of past ones.

Another argument for studying past experiences is to be found in how I argue that individuals, as actors in companies, draw upon previous experiences when they act: That is, the understanding of what happened is rationalized in hindsight, and we reinterpret past experiences, whereby the most recent picture we have becomes the one upon which is acted when we find ourselves in a new crisis situation.

<u>Focus on work, struggle to survive</u>

Now then, turning to the actual companies in my study, how, then, was I told that the crisis situations were dealt with?

A reporter recently asked me how the managers I interviewed went about keeping people motivated during such a severe crisis. I replied that it was hardly about motivation in this situation, those were not described as happy times. It was about keeping focus on work and struggling to survive, and keeping up morale as much as you could. The stories I was told were then about keeping up business and remaining focused, about attempts at keeping people calm and collected – all this in the middle of an extremely uncertain situation. The interviewees referred to how it was of utmost importance to create a sense of predictability and continuity in everyday life in spite of the uncertainty and the threat posed by the recession. This was done, they said, by sticking to certain things as much as possible, such as culture, strategies, social gatherings, and tradition in general.

Secondly, I was told that the fact that employees were able to stay active and focused depended on how the managers appeared to be in control even in the middle of an unpredictable environment. They managed this through actively drawing up plans and strategies as well as solutions to problems, although it was not possible to be certain of whether the solutions would actually apply. Nevertheless, someone had to assume responsibility and point out the direction so that a sense of order could be created in the chaotic situation, and the managers met the employees' expectations and did this. This helped employees maintain a sense of being in control of at least a part of everyday life, and thereby they avoided becoming paralyzed.

Thirdly, successful management during crisis was explained as being about keeping a balance between a hard and a soft side of managing. The managers would intervene in conflicts and emotionally charged situations, and did not hesitate to take difficult decisions: Problems were not swept under the mat, but dealt with at the earliest convenient time. On the other hand, I was told that the managers were at the same time experienced as very open and present and they were visibly participating in day-to-day business, people would even call them in the middle of the night for comfort. Handling this kind of balance is to a large extent a result of experience, I was told, and calls for the ability to improvise, intuitively knowing when to apply which strategy.

Furthermore, the interviewees claimed that good managers openly told the employees about the severity of the situation, which was extremely important for how people would be able to go on functioning. Knowing that the organization could be facing disaster was better than not being told anything, as this would have led to much speculation.

Good Management During A Crisis

What, then, constitutes good management in crisis? Several things were mentioned, among them predictability and consistency in behavior, sending clear messages, being capable of listening, openness, honesty, courage, presence, being genuine, and not complaining. Managers who had these qualities were respected and trusted, and were given much credit for the companies surviving the crisis by their subordinates.

The list sounds somewhat demanding, and the question of how the managers coped inevitably rises. They lived with the same amount of chaos and pressure as everyone else, one should think, but they were expected to be in charge and in control of events that could not be controlled that much. In addition, managers in general were often heavily critiqued by media, and illustrated as even cruel and inhuman. It was probably convenient to point them out as scapegoats.

The managers explained that a key to personal survival was not getting too involved in lamentations or problems of the individual employees. This did not mean that they were not human, but merely that they were able to set personal boundaries. The survival of the managers in severe organizational crises is, however, an issue that I find has been somewhat neglected, and is worthy of much more attention in the future. After all, my study does show that without the managers acting as they did in many cases, things would have been very different.

Imagining The Unthinkable

What can we learn from my study on a broader level? As I said in the beginning, managers often find themselves at loss for what to do when an unexpected crisis strikes. Living life planning for lightning to hit you, or in an organization, for turnover to drop by 50%, is obviously neither nice nor possible. However, imagining the unthinkable has become increasingly necessary. The recession our economy experienced in the 1990s has not and will not remain the last crisis that Finnish organizational life will experience.

APPENDIX: SUMMARY TABLE

Paradigms

- Accountants'
- Microeconomic
- Marketing
- Operations
- Technology
- Organizational
- Managerial Preferences

Positions

- Go For Gold
- Status Quo
- Tune Up
- Turnaround
- Exit

Principles

- Ethics
- Focus
- Excellence
- Frugality
- Urgency

CEO Characteristics

- Brains
- Guts
- Stamina

Turnaround Essentials

- Good numbers
- Competitive strength
- Customer goodwill
- Creditor co-operation
- Communications
- Managerial competency
- High functioning staff
- Prevention of calamities
- Urgency
- Board of directors / owner support
- Legality & ethics

Turnaround Phases

- Conservation of working capital
- Control of expenses
- Consolidation of progress
- Continuation or sale

Recurring Turnaround Themes

- Turkeys Don't Fly: Get The Right People
- The Big Bang: Pricing
- The Core Lubricant: Marketing
- The Thread That Binds: Communication
- Overhauling The Engine: Operations
- The River That Runs Through It: Strategy
- Shuffling The Deck: Financial Restructuring

APPENDIX: TURNAROUND CHRONOLOGY

Here is one example of many possible turnaround scenarios.

Quarters	1	2	3	4	5	6	7	8	9	10
Assess financial & cost accounting data	■									
Repricing of customer-products		■		■						
Meet banks	■	■	■	■	■	■				
Meet suppliers		■	■	■	■	■	■			
Meet customers			■	■	■	■	■	■	■	■
Meet staff - regular	■	■	■	■	■	■	■	■	■	■
Audits environmental, health & safety		■								
Review insurance, incl. Directors & Officers	■									
Brief board of directors	■	■	■	■	■	■	■	■	■	■
Cash budget	■	■	■	■						
Severance budget	■									
Terminations		■								
Stop the burn rate	■	■								
Close plants, divisions			■	■						
Expense control	■	■	■	■	■	■	■	■		
Establish asset productivity metrics		■	■	■						
Establish operating metrics		■	■	■						
Hire corporate, labor, environmental lawyers	■									
Assess executives & mangers		■	■							
Terminate executives & managers			■	■			■	■		
Cut dividends, owners' remuneration	■									
Start performance appraisals		■	■	■	■	■	■	■	■	■
Do customer-product contribution margin analysis		■								
Marketing - stop unproductive, unwise efforts	■	■	■							
Marketing - selective expenditures					■	■	■	■	■	■
Review channels of distribution			■	■	■	■				
Communications plan		■	■	■	■					
Operations: get grease under your fingernails	■	■	■	■	■	■	■	■	■	■
Purchasing - assess			■	■	■	■				
Proposal to creditors		■								
Negotiate new equity or debt					■	■	■	■		
R & D, special projects - assess, fix or close		■	■	■	■					
Strategy - evaluation		■	■	■						
Strategy - implementation				■	■	■	■	■	■	■
Maintain CEO mental & physical health	■	■	■	■	■	■	■	■	■	■

APPENDIX: THE POSITION QUIZ

The Position Quiz is a self-administered, diagnostic survey that indicates a company's possible Position. If a statement applies, circle the "Yes" to the right, even if there appears to be an overlap with previously circled items. If a statement does not apply, circle "No". To 'reach out and touch reality', take photocopies of the Quiz and ask key managers to complete the Quiz. Then, in a group meeting, compare responses: this could open the flow of meaningful discussion and start the process of building a consensus within the management team.

Worksheet: The Position Quiz

	Industry		
1	The industry is labor intensive.	B. Yes	B. No
2	Technical advances are being introduced in the industry fast, or primarily offshore.	B. Yes	B. No
3	Transportation costs to and from low wage countries are less than potential labor savings.	B. Yes	B. No
4	The industry has many small companies, lacking purchasing or marketing power or advanced inventory and information systems.	B. Yes	B. No
5	Big companies have started buying or squeezing out small companies.	B. Yes	B. No
6	The industry has production capacity surplus to normal demand.	B. Yes	B. No
7	A major customer or supplier is in receivership or bankruptcy or has a lengthy strike.	B. Yes	B. No
8	Decline in a product's social acceptability (ex. cigarettes, animal testing of cosmetics).	B. Yes	B. No
9	Government changes or plans to change the industry (includes regulation / deregulation, nationalization / privatization, removal of tariff / non-tariff barriers).	B. Yes	B. No
10	A major supplier or customer to the industry faces regulatory or international trade pressures.	B. Yes	B. No
11	Current or likely political turmoil may disrupt marketing, operations, key customers or key suppliers.	B. Yes	B. No
12	Commodity price fluctuations or currency fluctuations, which are not hedged.	B. Yes	B. No
13	A price war has started or is threatened.	B. Yes	B. No

14	Markets are volatile, or very cyclical.	B. Yes	B. No

	Strategy		
1	An expansion is a quantum leap forward, rather than an incremental advance.	B. Yes	B. No
2	The company has started a major strategic change without the human, technical, marketing and financial resources required.	B. Yes	B. No
3	An acquisition, capital expenditure, turnaround or strategic change is not working, and the answer appears to be spending more money.	B. Yes	B. No
4	The company plans to buy a business or to sell a division, and has not had professional advice.	B. Yes	B. No
5	The company has bought another business and does not really understand its strengths and weaknesses.	B. Yes	B. No
6	The company uses technology that is 2 yrs. older than its most aggressive competitor.	B. Yes	B. No
7	The company invests in technology for technology's sake, rather than to benefit customers, products or cost savings.	B. Yes	B. No
8	The company buys 'break-through' technology that its people are not trained thoroughly to use effectively.	B. Yes	B. No

	Shareholders		
1	There is a Shareholders' Agreement that was prepared and signed within 3 years.	A. Yes	A. No
2	Shareholders agree on all major aspects of the company's strategy and performance.	A. Yes	A. No
3	There is an effective Board Of Advisors or a Board Of Directors.	A. Yes	A. No
4	Wages to shareholders equal their market wages (what they would earn elsewhere).	A. Yes	A. No
5	The corporate owner or parent company is financially healthy.	A. Yes	A. No
6	Shareholders who work in the company are competent.	A. Yes	A. No
7	The company or shareholders have life insurance to buy a deceased shareholder's shares.	A. Yes	A. No

	Operations		
1	Purchasing is a senior management responsibility.	A. Yes	A. No
2	There is an on-going preventative maintenance program.	A. Yes	A. No
3	The plant / warehouse is very clean and orderly.	A. Yes	A. No

4	Movement of materials in the plant has been reduced by 25% within the last 2 yrs.	A. Yes	A. No
5	In-bound & out-bound freight was reduced as a per cent of sales by 20% within the last 2 yrs.	A. Yes	A. No
6	The order receipt / shipping cycle has been reduced by 25% within the last 2 years.	A. Yes	A. No
7	The company's key competitive strength is Operations.	A. Yes	A. No
8	Product quality, features and pricing have steadily improved.	A. Yes	A. No
9	Products lead or closely follow industry innovations.	A. Yes	A. No
10	Processes lead or closely follow the best industry practices.	A. Yes	A. No
11	The company earns a premium for its quality and service, either in pricing or volume of sales.	A. Yes	A. No
12	There has been a gradual shift from commodity products to value added products and services.	A. Yes	A. No
13	The company deleted, within the last 2 years, products or product categories based on their inadequate contribution to profits and growth potential.	A. Yes	A. No
14	The company has developed or acquired new products in the last two years.	A. Yes	A. No
15	Products introduced within the last five years account for more than 25% of total sales.	A. Yes	A. No
16	Scrap or rework costs are monitored and have decreased by 25% within the last 2 years.	A. Yes	A. No
17	Product costs, adjusted for quality and inflation, was steady or decreased within the last 2 yrs.	A. Yes	A. No
18	The company uses the most modern environmental standards in its manufacturing, warehousing, distribution and logistics.	A. Yes	A. No
19	The loss of a single supplier or class of supplier (e.g. computer chips) would cause a severe drop in sales, profits or cash flow.	B. Yes	B. No
20	Production schedules are revised sporadically by marketing staff.	B. Yes	B. No
21	Increased order-to-shipment time.	B. Yes	B. No
22	The company is reluctant to adopt new technology.	B. Yes	B. No
23	The person who manages the R & D function approves the R & D budget (common in companies established by an inventor or engineer).	B. Yes	B. No
24	The loss of a permit, license or certification (e.g. to handle uranium) would cause a severe drop in sales, profits or cash flow.	B. Yes	B. No
25	The company makes, uses or emits toxic or environmentally	B.	B.

	dangerous chemicals.	Yes	No
26	A key customer complains about quality or delivery.	B. Yes	B. No

	Marketing		
1	The company promptly responds to customer complaints.	A. Yes	A. No
2	The company tracks and analyzes patterns of customer complaints.	A. Yes	A. No
3	Marketing expenditures are based on contribution margins, not sales.	A. Yes	A. No
4	Marketing programs are adjusted annually, building on the strongest past practices and deleting unproductive historical expenditures.	A. Yes	A. No
5	The largest customer category represents less than 40% of total sales.	A. Yes	A. No
6	The largest customer represents less than 20% of total sales.	A. Yes	A. No
7	The company de-emphasizes or re-prices customers or classes of customers as a result of a thorough evaluation of their contribution to profits and their growth potential.	A. Yes	A. No
8	The company has a specific program to increase sales to high profit customers.	A. Yes	A. No
9	The company has targeted specific categories of new customers within the last two years.	A. Yes	A. No
10	The sales force is paid on contribution margin (not sales).	A. Yes	A. No
11	The company has developed a 'brand name' or high name recognition amongst its current and potential customers.	A. Yes	A. No
12	Contribution margin of each product or product group is calculated and used in marketing, production and inventory decisions.	A. Yes	A. No
13	Contribution margin of each customer or customer group is calculated and used in marketing, production and inventory decisions.	A. Yes	A. No
14	Company sales are growing faster than the total industry's sales.	A. Yes	A. No
15	Marketing is computerized (customer analysis, databases, telemarketing).	A. Yes	A. No
16	Sales are steady or declining slightly this fiscal year.	B. Yes	B. No
17	Sales decreased during the most recent two years.	B. Yes	B. No
18	Gross margin decreased this fiscal year.	B. Yes	B. No
19	Gross margin decreased during the most recent two years.	B. Yes	B. No

20	The sales force talks a lot about a competitor's new product or lower price.	B. Yes	B. No

	Finance		
1	Accounts receivable are steady or decreasing as a percent of sales.	A. Yes	A. No
2	Accounts receivable in dispute and credit vouchers are steady or decreasing as a percent of sales.	A. Yes	A. No
3	The cost accounting methodology has been thoroughly updated within 2 years.	A. Yes	A. No
4	The company uses cost accounting.	A. Yes	A. No
5	Accounting controls are strong and protect the company from fraud.	A. Yes	A. No
6	Management makes consistent efforts to prevent fraud.	A. Yes	A. No
7	Insurance policies have been reviewed and updated within 2 years.	A. Yes	A. No
8	Month-end statements are accurately completed within 25 days of month-end.	A. Yes	A. No
9	Year-end financial statements are completed within 45 days of year-end.	A. Yes	A. No
10	Bank covenants (e.g. margining of receivables) are consistently met.	A. Yes	A. No
11	Reports to the bank are complete, accurate and on time.	A. Yes	A. No
12	Management uses a rolling 4 - 6 months cash forecast to plan & control daily & monthly actions.	A. Yes	A. No
13	After-tax profits are at least twice dividends and reductions in shareholder loans.	A. Yes	A. No
14	Corporate goals determine what capital expenditures are approved.	A. Yes	A. No
15	Loans, receivables and payables with the company's subsidiaries or affiliates are paid / collected on normal trade terms.	A. Yes	A. No
16	After-tax income is at least twice interest expenses.	A. Yes	A. No
17	Cash management is a senior management responsibility.	A. Yes	A. No
18	The company prepares and uses a long-term capital expenditure plan and budget.	A. Yes	A. No
19	The company has a formal annual budget that is used to measure and reward success.	A. Yes	A. No
20	There is a monthly cycle count of inventory and comparison of units & costs to computer records.	A. Yes	A. No

21	Work-in-process inventories are valued accurately and consistently every month.	A. Yes	A. No
22	Sales have increased faster than inventory.	A. Yes	A. No
23	Sales taxes and payroll deductions are paid as required by legislation.	A. Yes	A. No
24	Property and business taxes are paid as required by legislation.	A. Yes	A. No
25	Payables are paid in accordance with suppliers' terms.	A. Yes	A. No
26	Year-end financial statements vary significantly from statements for the eleventh month.	B. Yes	B. No
27	The bank asks for more frequent reports.	B. Yes	B. No
28	The bank asks for additional security, especially supported personal guarantees.	B. Yes	B. No
29	Bank borrowings increased (except normal seasonal fluctuations) during the past year.	B. Yes	B. No
30	Shareholders invest (or, need to invest) more equity, by buying shares, increasing shareholder loans, or pledging personal assets.	B. Yes	B. No
31	Management was surprised within the last 12 months by a cash shortage.	B. Yes	B. No
32	High fixed costs in a cyclical business.	B. Yes	B. No
33	Overheads not readily linked to customer satisfaction or productivity.	B. Yes	B. No
34	Overheads increased in the most recent two years.	B. Yes	B. No
35	Investment in non-core activities, such as commercial real estate.	B. Yes	B. No
36	Profits before sales of fixed assets and extraordinary items decreased this fiscal year.	B. Yes	B. No
37	Profits before sales of fixed assets and extraordinary items decreased during the last two years.	B. Yes	B. No
38	Subsidiaries in industries or activities that are not closely related to the company's core business.	B. Yes	B. No
39	Inventory decisions are based on financial pressures or to increase financial ratios, not based primarily on customer needs and customer satisfaction analysis.	B. Yes	B. No
40	There are frequent (in the opinion of customers) stock-outs of high demand or critical items.	B. Yes	B. No
41	Suppliers restrict credit, or will only ship C.O.D.	B. Yes	B. No

	Technology		
1	The company uses technology in operations and logistics that is as modern and reliable as its leading competitor.	A. Yes	A. No
2	The company uses technology that is purchased from well-established vendors (as opposed to developing its own technology or relying on extensive customization).	A. Yes	A. No
3	The company has a documented plan to acquire and use technology to improve quality, cost efficiency and customer satisfaction.	A. Yes	A. No
4	Company executives are technically literate in application of technology to operations, marketing and administration.	A. Yes	A. No
5	Implementation of operations and logistics technology has been successful.	A. Yes	A. No

	People		
1	The company spends at least one week's pay per employee on training.	A. Yes	A. No
2	The company does semi-annual employee performance appraisals for all staff.	A. Yes	A. No
3	In a family business, the 'next generation' has worked three to five years elsewhere.	A. Yes	A. No
4	Employee absenteeism is low.	A. Yes	A. No
5	Employees are responsible, committed to excellence and have appropriate tools & training.	A. Yes	A. No
6	Poor performance is dealt with promptly - through training and coaching, or dismissal.	A. Yes	A. No
7	The company knows who the best employees are.	A. Yes	A. No
8	Key employees leave for reasons of job security or greater opportunities.	B. Yes	B. No
9	Increased staff and / or management turnover (typically the best leave first).	B. Yes	B. No
10	A unionized labor force strikes or threatens to strike.	B. Yes	B. No
11	A non-unionized labor force starts the certification process.	B. Yes	B. No

	Management		
1	There is a strong management team to handle growth, or the death of a key person.	A. Yes	A. No
2	Management receives and uses every month a one page financial summary of the key monthly trends that must be managed.	A. Yes	A. No
3	There is a clear organization chart, with identified responsibilities and authority.	A. Yes	A. No

4	Management has a sense of urgency appropriate to the issues.	A. Yes	A. No
5	Management has a sense of personal responsibility for the company's success (i.e. not relying on hope and good luck).	A. Yes	A. No
6	The company has a plan to recruit / train / promote people to replace senior management who may retire within 5 years.	A. Yes	A. No
7	There are weekly, focused, productive management meetings.	A. Yes	A. No
8	Senior management has noticeably increased its skills and sophistication within the last 2 years.	A. Yes	A. No
9	There is life and disability insurance on key executives.	A. Yes	A. No
10	There is a comprehensive, actionable business plan, prepared within 24 months, reviewed at quarterly Board of Directors / Advisors meetings.	A. Yes	A. No
11	The President develops a major non-business interest or activity, or dies.	B. Yes	B. No
12	The President undergoes a significant change, such as substance abuse, marital disruption or health problems.	B. Yes	B. No
13	The President focuses on his specialty, neglecting operations, marketing or finance.	B. Yes	B. No

Tally The Position Quiz

The table below lists the categories and the number of statements in the Position Quiz. Count the number of "A. No" and "B. Yes" that have been circled. Enter the scores in the table. The number of circles as a percent of the number of statements may indicate the company's most urgent challenges.

Worksheet: Tally The Position Quiz

Descriptions	Number	# of A. No	# of B. Yes	Total: A. No + B. Yes	Total– % of Descriptions
Industry	14				
Strategy	8				
Shareholders	7				
Operations	26				
Marketing	20				
Finance	41				
Technology	5				
People	11				
Management	13				
Total	145				

Graphing The Position Quiz

On the schematic below, mark the total number of "A. No" and "B. Yes" that have been circled. Join the numbers with a line. Draw lines, on either side of the first line, to show the possible range of Position. Companies may straddle two or even three positions. The difference between any two adjoining positions of the top four positions may be as simple as the trend. The simplest way to distinguish between two adjoining positions is to ask "Is my company getting better?" If the answer is yes, choose the higher position. If the answer is no, choose the lower position. Distinguishing between one of the top four positions and the Exit position should be influenced by the severity of the medium to long-term challenges compared to the adequacy of corporate resources.

Graphing The Company's Position

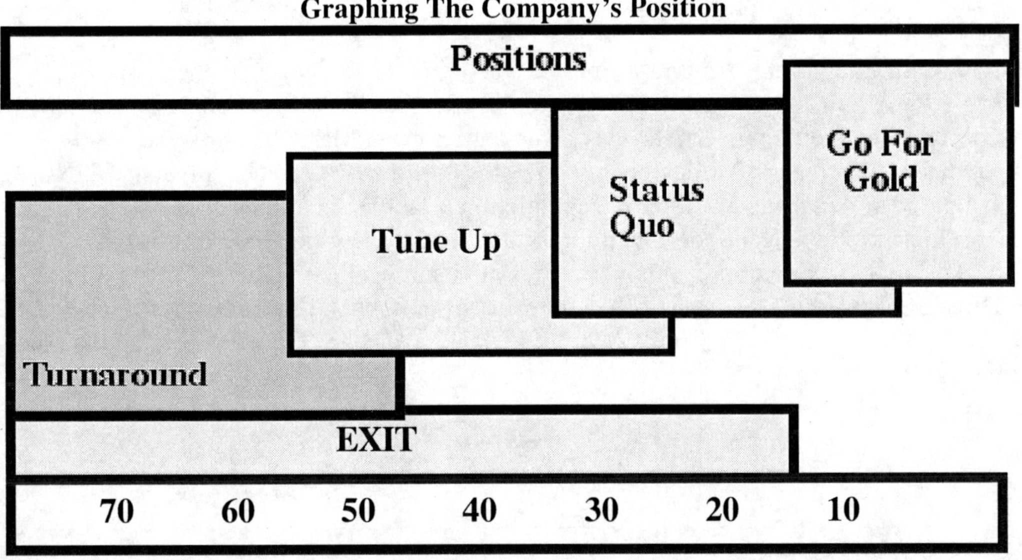

If the indicated position seems correct, it probably is; however, it is only a simple survey of issues that gives an estimate of a company's health. If the indicated Position seems wrong, the responses may have reflected an unduly positive or harsh perspective, or some issues, such as profits temporarily depressed by the launch of a new product, may be self-correcting in the near term, or the Quiz and the scaling of the five Positions may be incorrect or not be relevant to the company. Nonetheless, check the responses of other people in the company to validate any disagreement with the indicated Position.

APPENDIX: AUTHORS & ILLUSTRATORS

Profiles have been condensed from each author's and illustrator's resume or curriculum vita. For more information, contact the individual directly.

Alexandra Astafyeva

Alexandra Astafyeva, MBA
Ust-Kamenogorsk, Kazakhstan Email: alexaasta@mail.ru

Graduated from Kazakh-American Free University /KAFU/ (Ust-Kamenogorsk, Kazakhstan) with honors and BA in Economics and Management in 2003. As the top student of the graduating year she was given a grant from Marshall Christensen Foundation to pursue MBA degree in the USA, Northwest Nazarene University /NNU/ (Nampa, Idaho). During and after the completion of her studies she worked in the United States in marketing, event-coordination, PR and management. In 2005 returned to Kazakhstan and worked in its innovative business and banking industry. In 2008 became a Director of International Relations and Programs at KAFU. Fluent in Russian and English. Enjoys drawing portraits in black and white, designs clothes, sports, guitar and singing.

Crystal Dai

Crystal Dai
Toronto, Canada Email: dailin3395@hotmail.com

Crystal Dai was born in the People's Republic of China and immigrated to Canada. Currently, she is an art student in Toronto, Canada.

Stanley Winston Dermer

Stanley Winston Dermer, MD, FRCP(C)
Burlington, Ontario, Canada
drdermer@bellnet.ca www.drdermer.com

Education:
B.A., University of Ottawa, Ottawa, Ontario
1967 M.D., University of Ottawa, Ottawa, Ontario
1967 L.M.C.C. (Licentiate of Medical Council of Canada)
1967 Rotating Internship, St. Joseph's Hospital, Hamilton, Ontario
1968 – 1972 Resident, Dept. of Psychiatry, McMaster University, Hamilton, Ontario
1970 – 1971 Ontario Mental Health Foundation Traveling Fellowship at the Institute of Psychiatry (Maudsley and Bethlehem Royal Hospitals), University of London, U.K.
1971 – 1972 Chief Resident, Hamilton Psychiatric Hospital (Department of Psychiatry, McMaster University)

Professional Affiliations:
2005 – Present Special Advisor, Global Business and Economic Roundtable on Addiction and Mental Health Strategies
2005 – Present Advisor, Canadian Psychiatric Research Foundation
1981 – Present Hamilton Academy of Medicine
1973 – Present FRCP (C) Fellow of the Royal College of Physicians of Canada

Employment History – Clinical:
2003 – Present Principal, S.W. Dermer & Associates. Occupational Psychiatric Consultant. Medical Disability Management Consultation Services providing solutions to "complex" personnel problems often involving mental health issues
1996 – Present General Psychiatric Practice/Independent Medical Examinations (IME's)
1989 – 1996 President, BPS Programs Inc., A multidisciplinary rehabilitation program for motor vehicle accident victims; Independent Medical (Psychiatric) Examinations for Canada Pension Plan, insurance companies, corporate occupational health services, and Crown defense and plaintiff counsel
1982 – 1989 Co-founder and Executive Director for Hamilton Program for Schizophrenia; Hamilton, Ontario
1972 – 1982 Director, (Community) Social & Vocational Rehabilitation Program, Hamilton Psychiatric Hospital

Academic History:
1972 – 2006 Retired (2006), Associate Clinical Professor, Department of Psychiatry and Behavioural Neurosciences, McMaster University, Hamilton, Ontario

Brian K. Hunter

Brian K. Hunter, B.A. (Economics), MBA
Kitchener, Ontario, Canada
C: 519-721-7144 E: bdhunt@golden.net

Brian Hunter is currently Vice President Business Solutions with Spirited Investors, an innovative, community based, private equity firm located in Kitchener, Ontario that focuses on investing and acquiring small to medium sized businesses with unrealized potential.

Prior to this, he spent over 30 years with Roynat Capital as a Director and District Manager in Mississauga and Kitchener, Ontario, providing long term financing and merchant banking services focused on businesses with sales of $5 million to $250 million.

During his tenure with Roynat, he gained extensive experience in the areas of divestitures, acquisitions and restructurings involving underperforming companies. Brian accelerated the growth of numerous companies by providing long-term loans, mezzanine and equity capital, and financial advice. He led the recovery activities on numerous files through direct, day-to-day involvement with turnaround consultants, receivers, CCAA monitors, and other insolvency professionals.

Mr. Hunter earned his BA in Economics in 1974 and MBA from the University of Western Ontario in 1978, as well as completing Investment Management and Business Valuation courses at University of Toronto and University of Waterloo. He has written on a number of business topics in The Financial Post and Exchange Magazine.

He has served as President of the following organizations: Rotary Club of Kitchener-Conestoga, Western Business School Club of Waterloo Region, and the Mississauga Industrial Association.

Ann MacDiarmid

Ann MacDiarmid, HBA, ICD.D
Toronto, Ontario, Canada
416-567-6112 **raptor.comm@rogers.com**

Governance Experience:

- Director – UNICEF Canada, June 2002 to 2008.
- Advisor, 40 Oaks/Regent Park Redevelopment, 2007 to present
- Advisory Council – ClearView Strategic Partners, January 2004 to present.
- Governor - Offord Centre for Child Studies, May 2000 to 2004.
- Trustee – Superior Propane Income Trust, 1996 to 2000.
- Board Member – Grey Cup 2000 (1998-2000), Calgary 2010 Winter Olympic Bid (1997-1999), Calgary Expo 2005 World's Fair International Relations Committee (1996-1997), Carleton University Development Corporation (1994-1996), Ottawa Carleton Economic Development Corporation (OCEDCO) (1994-1996), Regional Economic Diversification Opportunities (REDO) (1994-1996).
- Founding Member/Chair – Ottawa Carleton Entrepreneurship Centre (1994-1996), Licensing Executive's Society, Canada's Capital Region (1990-1991), Emergency Food Box Program (1990-1996).

Professional Experience:

- Raptor Communications, President/Consultant – crisis communications, senior executive speech writing & coaching 1993-present
- Workplace Safety and Insurance Board of Ontario (WSIB) 2002-2003
- Vice President of Marketing and Communications
- FGI – formerly CHC Working Well, Director of Marketing 2000-2001
- University of Calgary, Director of Marketing 1998-2000
- TELUS Advanced Communications, Director of Marketing 1996-1998
- EXPO Canada 2005, Chief Executive Officer 1994-1995
- Pegasus Publishing, President 1992-1993
- Canadian Intellectual Property Management Corporation 1990-1994
- Canadian Association of Paediatric Hospitals (CAPH) 1989-1990
- Botsford Ketchum Inc., San Francisco 1977-1979
- Procter & Gamble Company of Canada 1974-1977

Education:

- Honors Business Administration, University of Western Ontario, 1974.
- University of Lausanne, Canadian Junior College, Lausanne Switzerland, 1970.
- Succeeding in the Boardroom, Schulich School of Business, York University, 2003.
- Rotman School of Business, University of Toronto, Institute of Corporate Directors Corporate Governance College, 2004, Accredited director, 2004.

Peter McCann

Peter McCann, Dipl.A.A., MBA, ICD.D.
Hamilton, Canada
905.973.1551

pmccann@globalserve.net **pmccann@mccaconsultants.com**
www.trafford.com/00-0060.html **www.mccaconsultants.com**

Business History

Chair of Management Team (CEO), Benson Chemicals Limited.	Sept.05 – Feb.08
Chair of Board of Directors, Benson Chemicals Limited.	Jan.02 – Feb.08
McCann Corporate Consulting Associates, Hamilton, Canada.	Nov.89 - current
Predecessors to KPMG, Hamilton & Kitchener, Canada.	Apr.88 - Nov.89
Roynat Capital, Ottawa, Montreal and Hamilton, Canada.	Apr.77 - Aug.86
IDB / FBDB / BDC, Ottawa, Canada.	Jun.75 - Apr.77

Directorships & Memberships

The Institute of Corporate Directors, member.	2002 - 2008
Turnaround Management Association, member.	2008
The Canadian International Council, Hamilton Chapter – Director.	2001 - 2003
The Canadian International Council – member.	2000 - 2008
Chair, Board of Directors, Benson Chemicals Limited.	2002 - 2008
Hamilton Chamber of Commerce.	1989 - 2008
Director of the Board of a hospitality industry company.	1999 - 2000
The Canadian Club of Hamilton, member	1995 - 2008
Fundraising Cabinet, United Way of Burlington & Hamilton-Wentworth.	1991-1992

National, International & Cross-Cultural Experience

Canada: Worked / consulted in seven of ten provinces.	1989 - 2008
First Nations: Consulted on four First Nations in Canada.	1994-2006
United States: Consulted in Pennsylvania, Washington, D.C.	1993, 2003
Kazakhstan: Visiting professor.	1998, 1999, 2000
Azerbaijan: Visiting professor.	2001 and 2002
Russia: Visited St. Petersburg.	2003 and 2004
Finland: Advisory meetings in Helsinki	2008

Education

Harvard Business School, Harvard University, Negotiation course	2006
Institute of Corporate Directors Accredited as ICD. D.	2004
Richard Ivey School of Business, Un. of Western Ontario, MBA	1988

Rick Morgan

Rick Morgan, BA (Economics)
Hamilton (Ancaster), Ontario, Canada
T. 905-631-4436 E. **stratdirect@cogeco.ca**

Overview:

- With over three decades of working in the disciplines of marketing, communications, research and planning at advertising agencies on behalf of clients, Rick has developed a solid, strategic perspective. He is committed to providing clear, pragmatic advice to guide marketing and communications planning based on the "facts of the marketplace".
- His experience in working across a broad diversity of sectors and challenges has given Rick a wealth of knowledge with which to tackle client problems.
- His skill sets include creative problem-solving, focus group moderating (hundreds of sessions over the years), brand and creative planning, as well as complete facility with all available research tools and methods.
- Many of Rick's clients represent long-standing relationships – clients who recognize the tangible, value-added contribution he provides. Indeed, for many organizations, Rick has consulted on an ongoing basis as their de facto market research director or marketing communications advisor.

Career History:

- Strategic Direction, Business Builders ROI, ConnectID: Nov. 2003 to present, Senior Consultant and Partner
- InsightGroup, Mississauga: November 2001 to November 2003, Senior Consultant
- Grey Worldwide Research Division, consulting on Grey and Kelley Advertising clients
- Kelley Advertising, Hamilton: February 1999 to November 2001, Vice President, Strategic Services, reported to President
- Grey Worldwide, Toronto: May 1994 to February 1999, Vice President Strategic Services, reported to CEO & President, member of Executive Committee
- Kelley Advertising, Hamilton: prior to May 1994, Vice President, Research & Strategic Planning, reported to CEO & President; career path during tenure: Account Executive, Media Manager, Research Director, VP, Shareholder, Director & Officer of the Company

Education:

- BA Economics, McMaster University
- Certified Advertising Agency Practitioner (ICA)
- Synectics Creative Problem-solving, Cambridge, Massachusetts

Mia Örndahl

Mia Örndahl, Ph.D.
Helsinki, Finland
mia.orndahl@paxtraining.fi 011-358-40-709 6848

Mia Örndahl holds an MA and a PhD and she was previously a researcher at the Department of Management and Organization at Hanken in Helsinki. While conducting her research, she also facilitated corporate training programs on group dynamics, team learning and conflict management. She has worked a private consultant and lecturer in crisis management and crisis communication for several years. Mia has also served as a volunteer for the Primary Care Unit of the Finnish Red Cross in Helsinki.

Mia's PhD thesis, which she completed in 2005, is on the survival stories of Finnish companies that successfully recovered from the economic recession of the early 1990s. The thesis focuses on how managers dealt with the uncertainty and how business was conducted under unstable and unfamiliar circumstances. It portrays the social aspects of communication and leadership in a crisis context, and describes the working environment of the case companies in practice.

Her training and consulting company is specialized in facilitation as a means for handling management and communication in large-scale organizational changes as well as conflicts and offers workshops and consulting on these topics. The purpose of the services is to give managers and other key individuals facilitation methods to handle crisis situations, change processes and conflicts. Clients are provided with a basic understanding of how human beings respond to changes and crises. They thereby learn how to cope with the task of managing personnel, and to act so as to create a sense of continuity and security in their everyday work despite the situation and future being uncertain. How should managers and supervisors act in order to preempt the emergence of unnecessary disruptions such as conflicts and other problems that hinder business from being kept up and running, and that staff remain focused and active?

Other main purposes are to learn how to communicate difficult issues, and how to avoid the personnel becoming paralyzed through making sure that communication is carried out correctly and timely.

Clients thereby acquire the capability to deal with and resolve conflicts and other issues, which change processes and crisis situations can lead to, so that business operations can continue uninterrupted.

J. Keith Robson

J. Keith Robson, B.Sc. (Hons), ICD.D.
Tel: (905) 628-9535 Cell: (416) 417-4961
Email: **jkrobson@sympatico.ca** Website: www.jkrassoc.com

Professional History:

JKR & ASSOCIATES INC., President & CEO *Current*

HAMILTON PORT AUTHORITY 2002 – 2007

President & CEO

Institute of Corporate Directors, President & CEO, *2001-2002*

ASTON ROBSON INTERNATION INC. 1996 – 2003

Strategic management consultant with short and long term assignments

CP TRUCKS/INTERLINK FREIGHT SYSTEMS 1993 – 1996

President & CEO

LINWOLD MANAGEMENT INC *1990-1993*

VARITY CORPORATION 1972 – 1990

A holding company, with worldwide sales of US$3.5 billion, including the Massey Ferguson Group, Perkins Engines, Dayton Walther and Kelsey Hayes. Roles included: President, Aftermarket Parts Business 1988 – 1990, Vice President, International Services 1987 – 1988, Vice President, Comptroller and Planning 1983 – 1987, Director, Business Planning; Director, Product Planning 1978 – 1983, and Director, Product Planning, and Director, Marketing Planning of Perkins Engines Ltd., (UK Subsidiary of Varity) 1972 – 1978

CHRYSLER UK/Europe

Product Planning and Marketing 1967 – 1972

Education:

- B.Sc. (Hons.) University of Aston, Birmingham, UK. President of the Guild of Students.
- Institute of Marketing (UK) courses in Marketing, Economics.
- Directors Program, Richard Ivey Business School.
- Certified Graduate of the ICD Corporate Governance College, Rotman Business School
- Numerous industry seminars and training courses.

Fred S. Wagman, CA
Toronto, Ontario Canada
T: 416.922.7972 C: 416.520.2874 E: **frwagman@rogers.com**

Professional History:

Fred S. Wagman Consultants 1997- Current

The consultancy provides operational and financial consulting services to owner-managed businesses of all sizes including manufacturing, wholesaling, services and professionals. Consulting services includes turnarounds, acting both on behalf of the lender and the borrower, and executive coach and mentor to both owner-managers and senior corporate executives.

Kadoke Display Limited 1993-1997

COO and CFO of a company that provided custom built exhibits for trade shows to customers both in Canada and internationally. Manufacturing facilities were located in Canada and in Europe.

Lanzarotta Wholesale Grocers 1987-1993

VP Operations and Finance of a wholesale grocer servicing independently owned retailers in the Greater Toronto area, with sales in excess of $700 million.

Weiss, Wagman & Rowan 1966-1987

Partner/Managing Partner of charter accountancy firm.

Other Activities

Volunteer at Rotman School of Business, University of Toronto to MBA Program.
Member of TEC Associate Group
Volunteer and Board member for various charitable organizations.
Member of various Canadian Institute of Chartered Accountants' committees.

ISBN 142519099-5
9 781425 190996